Practic

GARDEN
FEATURES

Yvonne Rees

The Crowood Press

First published in 1995 by
The Crowood Press Ltd
Ramsbury, Marlborough
Wiltshire SN8 2HR

British Library Cataloguing-in-Publication Data

A catalogue record for this book is available from the British
Library.

ISBN 1 85223 856 9

Dedication
For my husband who actually constructs these things.

Picture Credits
Line-drawings by Claire Upsdale-Jones
All photographs are by Sue Atkinson except for the following:
those on pages 1, 8 (right), 11 (right), 19 (left), 20, 37, 43, 48
(left) and 59 (left) are by the author; that on pages 2/3 is by
Rokes Ltd; that on page 27 is by Dobies Seeds; that on page 31
is by Jessica Houdret; that on page 52 is by Suttons Seeds; and
that on page 53 is by Ian Murray.

Acknowledgements

Typeset in Optima by Chippendale Type Ltd,
Pool-in-Wharfedale, West Yorkshire
Printed and bound by Paramount Printing Group, Hong Kong
Colour Separation by Next Graphic Limited, Hong Kong.

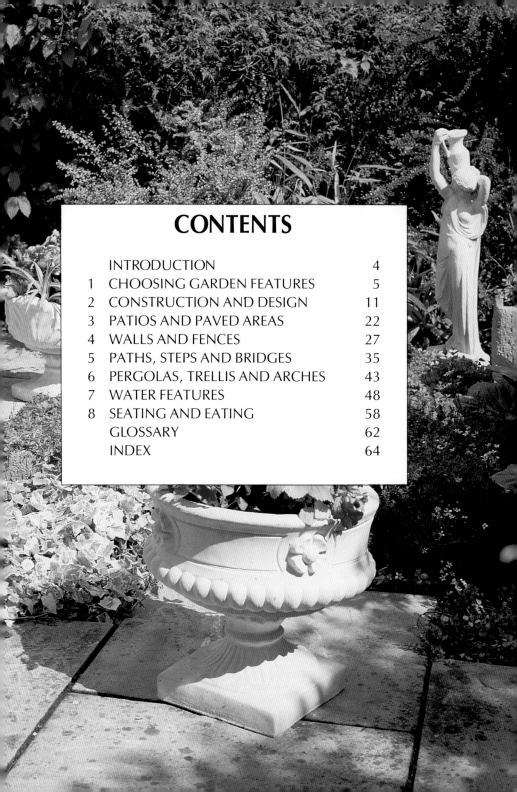

CONTENTS

INTRODUCTION

It is the hard landscaping features – the paths and paving, fences, screens, trellis, pools and pergolas – that make up the bare bones, the framework of your patio or garden plan. They may seem to take secondary place when the plants become established and begin to soften and partially disguise the basic skeleton; but if you get this framework right you are two-thirds of the way to a successful scheme. These are the features that shape your plot, that create clever optical illusions by apparently altering the length and width of a less than perfect site. They also satisfy your practical requirements in the garden, by providing shade and privacy, a dry, level surface under foot for furniture, or access to and across different features. Trellis, arches, pergolas and tunnels can add height and interest to the area and supply a decorative framework for climbing or trailing plants. With properly planned paved areas, paths and supportive or protective structures, the garden starts to work for you on a practical level as well as satisfying the sensual pleasures of sight and scent. If the framework is sound, you will find regular maintenance tasks will be easier too.

The concept of 'garden rooms', where you create different areas within the garden for eating, relaxing, different seasonal interest and so on, relies on hard landscaping features to provide shape and character. While the choice of plants is important, it can be your choice of features that will stamp a particular style and theme on a garden: the random effect of a country cottage, for example, with a winding herring-bone brick path and rustic arch; or an oriental atmosphere conjured up by a patio styled like a Japanese tea garden with stepping-stones and areas of sand and gravel. Your choice of materials is equally important for creating a certain look and style: a predominance of stone and brick can create a very formal look, while timber is softer and has more rustic associations. Whatever

you choose, the planning and installation of just one successful hard landscaping feature – a fine patio, a stunning pergola, or perhaps a raised pool – can transform your garden and give it a professional touch.

However, whether you are considering a total redesign or simply a new feature for your garden, it can be a daunting prospect to know where to start if you are not a professional builder or joiner. Yet once you learn a few basic techniques, even the more elaborate looking features can be quite simple for the amateur to construct. Specialist tools can be hired or borrowed if necessary. There are also a great many structures and surfaces you can buy ready-made from your local garden centre, which simply need assembling. If you are determined to tackle the project yourself, or even if you intend to employ a professional to do the job for you, it helps to know what is entailed when choosing a particular style and size of feature. This book will show you just a few of the possibilities and hopefully will inspire you to do something creative with your own garden. Chapter by chapter you will learn the creative and practical options for boundaries, patios, pergolas, trellis and built-in features like seating, raised beds and barbecues. Whatever size garden or back yard you have, most of these ideas can be adapted to suit. In a large garden, these features are useful for dividing the plot up into smaller areas; on little more than a patio, they are essential for adding interest and creating the impression of extra space. Nor should you let budget cramp your style: second-hand materials and an original idea can be far more exciting than something you bought from a shop, and will give an instant sense of maturity to the garden. Whether you use this book for inspiration or instruction, it is important to maintain that feeling of originality and to put your personal stamp on the features in your garden, the same way you would with an interior design within the home.

1 • CHOOSING GARDEN FEATURES

There are various factors that will affect your choice of garden features. You will be limited by the size and shape of your plot, and by its boundaries and orientation. Sometimes you will want to disguise the shape, where it seems too long or narrow for example. Making your basic plan run diagonally across the plot, or breaking it up with a winding path between features helps to distract attention from the furthest boundary. Even better is to use screens or trellis to break up the garden across its width and to make sure you cannot see the plot all in one view. That element of mystery, of secret areas unseen, gives the impression of greater size. Where the garden is rather large and boring, you can use the same methods to add interest by breaking it up into smaller areas linked by circuitous paths, bridges and stepping-stones. Again, some of these can be made secret by screening from view.

A simple gazebo construction makes an instant focal point and provides excellent support for climbing plants.

A sunken patio would make an exciting and unusual feature where there is a natural hollow or depression in the garden. It would offer instant shelter and seclusion and would be cheaper than landfilling and levelling.

Another way you can distract the eye from the true boundaries of your garden is to create a focal point, such as a statue, a sundial or even a small summer-house, and position it where it will attract the maximum attention: in the centre of a lawn or patio perhaps, or at the end of a long vista bordered by plants or trees.

Sometimes the shape of a plot may suggest a feature: you can straighten up an L-shaped building with a pool or patio. A garden of too regular a shape can be made more interesting by not positioning features parallel to the boundaries, but installing them at right angles and using informal shapes and designs. The route between one feature and another will suggest the best place for paths; make the plan more interesting by not taking the direct route, but meandering through the garden to encourage a more leisurely, contemplative pace. Once paths have been planned, you will see immediately where to position your features.

Boundaries of Taste

A country site will probably want to incorporate the view beyond the garden into a kind of distant vista. Here the boundaries will be unobtrusive, something low or open like ranch-style fencing. Where protection from prevailing winds is required, the open countryside can be screened with something informal like a hedgerow, a drystone wall or rustic fencing.

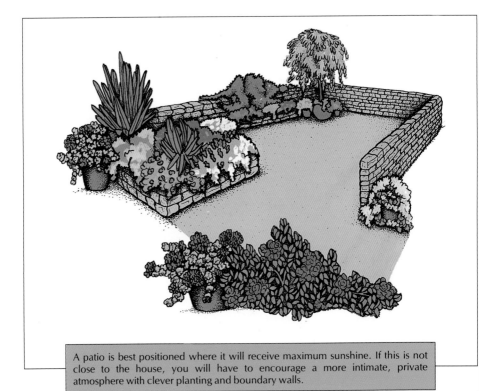

A patio is best positioned where it will receive maximum sunshine. If this is not close to the house, you will have to encourage a more intimate, private atmosphere with clever planting and boundary walls.

The town garden generally prefers privacy and often there is a less than attractive view to be hidden. Here the walls and fences are high, solid and substantial, preferably strong enough to take the weight of trellis and climbing plants for added interest. Tall boundaries will dictate the layout of the rest of the garden as they create both shade and shelter.

Orientation – the direction of sunshine through the day – is also an important consideration when planning the type and position of landscaped features. Patios and summer-houses, for example, should be positioned where they will receive maximum sunshine, even if this is at the opposite end of the garden from the house. You may even consider having more than one patio, for different times of day and different purposes: a lounging area partially shaded by a pergola at the end of the garden if this is the warmest, sunniest position; another paved area complete with outdoor lighting and built-in barbecue close to the house for evening entertaining.

Assessing the Plot

If your garden is raw and new, or presents you with a neglected wilderness with no existing features worth saving, it will be a blank canvas on which to plot your chosen landscape. You can take a piece of graph paper, position your plot on it to scale and play around with the kind of features you would like to include cut out of card or paper. Provided you adhere to the factors already discussed, the resulting design will be limited only by your budget and imagination.

An existing mature garden is a different matter; there will be various features already installed, some of which you will want to keep, others which stand in the way of your plans. Always think carefully before you remove or destroy anything, especially

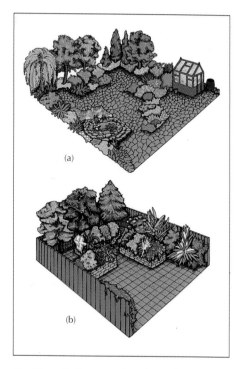

(a)

(b)

Deciding whether to enclose the garden or leave it more open plan will influence the whole look and atmosphere of your garden.
(a) This garden immediately feels more informal, yet remains easy to maintain thanks to large areas of decorative paving rather than lawn, and a good backdrop of trees, shrubs and perennials. Annuals provide seasonal colour.
(b) This layout is more formal and is better suited to an urban location. Trees have been restricted to small species which do not grow much taller than 3m (10ft) and can offer several points of interest such as attractive flowers, foliage, bark and autumn colour.

if it is an established tree or shrub that may take years to replace. If an existing feature is in the right place but you do not like the style, it may be possible to update or transform it, for example by resurfacing a patio with timber decking or new slabs. Ugly walls and fences can be disguised with screens or trellis covered in climbing plants. You must remember that removing a major feature will cost time and money.

Personal Style

As well as the practical elements that will influence your initial choice of garden feature, there are also personal reasons why you will ultimately choose a certain type and style of feature. Foremost will be personal preference, the kind of garden features

Wisteria is a woody stemmed climber grown primarily for its superb hanging racemes of heady-scented mauve, purple or white flowers. It is perfect for sunny walls and pergolas or for growing against a building. Here the pergola effect of a flowery walkway has been created without the need for a structure at all as the woody stems have been trained on wires to form a series of archways. Wisteria needs a rich, well-drained soil and mulching around the roots. It should be pruned after flowering and again before growth starts in the spring to encourage plenty of blooms.

Front gardens need good design too. They must appear welcoming yet remain easy to maintain, like this cosy paved area which uses old materials for a traditional atmosphere and evergreens for a leafy backdrop.

that appeal to you and your life-style. Chosen carefully, your garden or patio will start to take on a certain character where features have a similar style or compatibility. It helps if you have a clear idea, before any major construction or installation takes place, of the kind of style or atmosphere you are hoping to create. Often this will naturally mimic that of your choice of interior

decorations and furnishings and this can be very effective, not only encouraging a sense of continuity in the home, but also blurring the boundaries between inside and outside as you move from one to the other. This can make both home and garden seem more spacious than they really are, which can be a real asset where space is limited. To encourage and reinforce this effect, plan leafy interior areas such as conservatories or sunrooms which open naturally on to partially furnished outdoor areas such as patios and courtyards.

To a large extent, the materials you use to build your features will dictate the look and style. Well-weathered second-hand timber, rough-cut wood or unpeeled bamboo poles or chestnut create a definite country cottage atmosphere for those looking for an informal garden. Use these to create trellis or rustic arches for the proverbial rambling roses to smother; they also make charmingly uneven fencing or even bench seats and rough tables. For other areas, you can buy woven willow screens to maintain that country look. When it comes to paving for paths or patios, you will be considering old stone slabs or setts, or brick for creating old-fashioned herring-bone or weave patterns. Again, second-hand materials look best, giving an instantly mature look with their uneven colouring and surface. Use cobbles to create a change of texture on the patio; log slices to make rustic stepping-stones across the lawn or areas of mulching wood chips; and railway sleepers to edge borders or raised beds.

Unusually, this garden has few hard landscaping features, but combines a dense patchwork of plant material linked by paths and steps.

For the town or city home, a formal garden is often more in keeping. Both garden and patio can be landscaped to a strictly geometric design, based on a series of interlocking circular, square and rectangular shapes. Here, regular slabs, paviors and new brick can be used to create all kinds of smart features, often employing a mixture of materials for variety and interest. Matching materials to those used to build the house or a nearby outbuilding helps to encourage a sense of continuity and formality. The formal garden likes to create built-in complexes: a patio including a raised pool, integral seating, raised beds, maybe a built-in barbecue. Often features will be on several levels to add height and interest to the area. Timber is sawn and well finished, maybe even painted and varnished in natural or subtle colours, and is used to create perfect pergolas, platforms, maybe even timber-decked areas and walkways for a change of texture from the hardness of stone and concrete. Pavers for paths and patios come in all shapes, sizes and colours, some of which imitate natural stone, while others are definitely ornamental. You can buy interlocking shapes which can be used to create an infinite variety of patterns and designs for patios, small walls, raised beds and integrated features. To add height and

provide a framework for elegant climbers, you can also buy decorative metal arches, hoops and gazebo structures. Use several of these creatively for screening or for covered walkways in conjunction with climbing plants.

The more adventurous might enjoy the challenge of creating an oriental garden, or at least designing a corner of the garden with an oriental atmosphere. Here the hard landscaping features are crucial to the overall design, the addition of a few architectural plants such as bamboo, mosses and dwarf maples being merely an ornament. Natural rock, stones, sand and pebbles are used to great effect, primarily to represent nature as miniature seas, plains and mountain ranges. Many oriental gardens incorporate pools or a moving water feature, such as a fountain or water spout. Although the basic plan is formally laid out, the final effect is very natural.

The Right Garden for You

Another personal factor that will influence

To soften the effect of an expanse of paving and create the right atmosphere anywhere in the garden, plant containers and ornaments are your exterior design accessories. Closely clipped evergreens like these are the perfect combination of plant and decoration.

your choice and design of features is your life-style. If you like to spend much of your leisure time in the garden, relaxing and entertaining, a patio, or several patio areas, will be of primary importance. You can justify giving plenty of space to paved areas and incorporating a wide range of additional features such as seating, a barbecue, maybe a built-in spa or hot tub. Screening for shade and privacy will be important.

Alternatively, if you are more interested in the plants, you will want plenty of arches and trellis for climbing plants, an easy-to-negotiate path that takes a long and leisurely route around and between different planting areas, and maybe screens to divide the garden into sections for growing different kinds of plant.

The kind of garden you need if you have very little leisure time is different again: it must be quick and easy to maintain, so hard

landscaping features will play a dominant part in the design. A well-designed combination of raised beds, water features and paved areas leaves you free to enjoy the garden and not consider it a chore.

In the family garden, you will have to include features with children in mind. A pond or pool is not recommended for children under five years of age, but there is no reason why you should not have a small bubble fountain or a wall spout trickling into a hidden reservoir. The children will appreciate a decent system of paths for riding bicycles, but you will need to provide a good edging to beds and borders such as kerbstones or stout timber, or even build raised beds, to protect your plants. Sand-pits, paddling pools and bunker storage for outdoor toys can be incorporated into built-in patio features, whether set in concrete, timber-decking or pavers.

2 • CONSTRUCTION AND DESIGN

You will already have some idea of the combination of features you would like to see in your garden or back yard. Most people would give priority to some kind of patio, for example, but how big, what shape and what style? There are various elements that can be selected to suit your own particular life-style, as outlined in Chapter 1: a rose arch, a barbecue, maybe a sand-pit for the children. A quick sketch to scale on a piece of graph paper will soon show how many you can fit into your plot. For inspiration on style and design, however, or even for good ideas on hard landscaping features, it helps to browse through the pictures in a book or to go to one of the major garden shows, notebook in hand. It is also a good idea to visit your local garden centre or builder's yard and see exactly what materials are available. The opportunity to handle slabs, bricks,

Bricks can be used to create highly ornamental effects.

timber and paviors is invaluable for acquainting yourself with the different finishes and textures, and this will make choices easier when you come to draw up the final plan. It also helps to make a note of sizes and costs: this will not only give you some idea of what can be done, but will also be invaluable when budgeting and ultimately when ordering materials. It is essential that you work out accurately what you need, so always double check your calculations and measurements.

Concrete

Concrete can be a versatile and relatively inexpensive medium for garden features and, if properly mixed and correctly laid, will provide an extremely strong and long-lasting surface. It is mixed from cement, sand, an aggregate such as small stones or shingle, and water, to a ratio of one part cement to two parts sand and three parts aggregate. To calculate how much concrete you need for a job, you should measure the square area and multiply it by the depth. Add about ten per cent to this cubic measurement to allow for wastage. A bucket or

A simple paved area may be extended to include steps, walls and other features.

Do not be afraid to combine a whole range of features and materials within your garden scheme.

The area must be prepared before concreting, as described for individual features in this book, then a temporary framework of wooden shuttering erected like a mould, so that the concrete can be poured on in a continuous motion for a smooth finish. If you soap the shuttering planks first, they slip out more easily after the concrete has started to set. After laying, the surface should be smoothed with a plank; you can achieve a finer finish by tamping the board towards the edge, but this does risk weakening the cement. After about four hours, the concrete can be smoothed to a finer finish by using a float; or if you want a rougher finish for a patio, brushing with a soft broom adds a texture.

Concrete can be used successfully for

barrow can be used to measure the parts accurately and care should be taken that no dirt or debris is allowed to get into the mix or this will affect its setting properties. There are proprietary additives such as colourants, waterproofers and anti-frost chemicals that can be added at the mixing stage: the colourants are usually used to make a patio area look a little less stark; the waterproofer and anti-frost additives are particularly useful when concrete-lining a pool.

You can mix the concrete by hand, but for anything other than the smallest of jobs, an electrical or petrol-driven mixer is recommended. These can be hired by the day or weekend and it is important that you have everything ready for the day you have booked so that you can get your money's worth. The water is used to bind the other ingredients into a stiff paste: if it is too sloppy it will be difficult to work with, especially if lining a pool where you will find the concrete tends to slump to the bottom. If possible, do not attempt concreting in extremes of weather: heat, sun or rain. You will have to cover the area with a plastic sheet or tarpaulin after you have finished if there is any risk of rain or frost.

The aromatic herb thyme (*Thymus*) includes a choice of attractive prostrate forms which are ideal for growing at the base of architectural features, in pockets of soil on stone walls, in stone or pebble gardens and even in the cracks between bricks and paving slabs. They prefer a light sandy soil and a sunny position which will encourage a carpet of tiny fragrant flowers to bloom in summer. Treading on thyme only encourages it to flourish and to release its familiar oily scent as you pass. It does not like waterlogged soil or cold winds. Cutting back after flowering will prevent the plant growing straggly. Green leaved *Thymus praecox* and the greyer *T. pseudolanuginosus* are both suited to paving areas.

Decorative patio blocks are useful for building small ornamental walls or inserting decorative sections within a larger boundary wall.

paths and patios, sunken and raised pools, sand-pits and hard-standing for sheds and summer-houses, gazebos and stores. If you think it might look a little plain and attract glare when used over the large surface of a patio, the mixture can be coloured as mentioned earlier. Alternatively you can brush the surface with a broom while still wet, leave for about eight hours until it starts to set, then brush it again and hose it down. This produces a more textured surface. Or you might sprinkle shingle or chippings on to the concrete while it is still wet to introduce a little interest. The most creative option is to buy or hire special pattern blocks which, when stamped on the wet concrete, produce reasonably convincing patterns and designs imitating paving slabs, bricks, stones or cobbles. These options not only look more decorative but also provide a less slippery surface when the concrete is wet.

Paving Slabs

Although paving slabs are primarily intended for patios, they can make excellent paths or, partially sunk into the grass, stepping-stones or a pool surround. You might also use them to create built-in seating or other features on the patio to maintain a matching finish. Paving slabs are available in many shapes, sizes and finishes, according to how much you are prepared to pay. The most expensive can be virtually indistinguishable from real stone. Others are designed to be interlocking so that you can create an infinite variety of patterns and designs.

To lay slabs, you will have to position about 2.5cm (1in) of mortar on to the prepared area; remember when excavating to allow for all the layers plus the thickness of the slabs. The mortar should be levelled

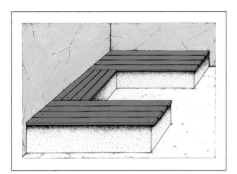

Built-in bench seating could be an integral part of your patio construction.

Bricks

Bricks are surprisingly versatile in the garden for creating not just walls, but many attractive yet practical features. Old second-hand bricks are perfect for a mellow, old-fashioned informal feel, while new bricks with their wide range of shades from russet and buff to yellow and blue, can be used to

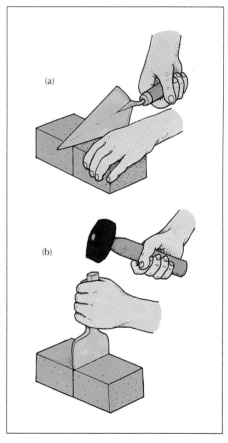

Cutting bricks. (a) Use a broad blade to make a groove along the cutting line. (b) Place a chisel in the groove and give it a sharp blow with a mallet or bricklayer's hammer.

with a screed board and gently pressed down. The alternative is to dab mortar on to the back of each slab: a dab on each corner and one in the centre. You normally start laying slabs in the top left-hand corner using battens as a guideline. Each slab should be positioned carefully, checking with a spirit-level that it is straight and not likely to tilt or rock. Tap down lightly using a piece of timber to soften the blow and prevent cracking the slab. A straight-edge will ensure that each slab is level with the next. This is important as any unevenness will create puddles when it rains.

Continue working along the first row, checking each slab is straight and level before moving on to the next, until all the complete slabs have been laid. Then cut and lay all the missing part-slabs in one go. Ideally, you should plan the patio so that no cutting is necessary, but this is not always possible. You will need an angle-grinder to cut the slabs. Again, these can be hired from specialist tool shops. You can butt the slabs together or space them about 1cm (½in) apart. A piece of timber batten used as a guide will help to keep the spaces regular. The gaps between can later be filled with smoothed mortar or simply filled with sand or soil to allow creeping plants to grow and soften the edges of the pavers.

create really smart formal features from patio paving and paths, to raised beds, pools and built-in barbecues. It is important that you use only hard bricks in the garden because these will be able to withstand frosts. There is nothing worse than spending time and money on an elaborate feature and seeing the whole thing shattered and ruined after a single cold season.

If you are building walls, it is essential to check that the bricks are level by using a suspended cord line. The bricks are laid using a concrete mortar mix and are over-lapped so that the joins are staggered; this is what gives the wall its strength and stability. There are various patterns and designs you can create simply by controlling the position of the brick against its neighbour and each will affect the strength and appearance of the wall. Walls can also be 'single' or 'double' skin or leaf, that is one or two bricks deep, and again this will affect the wall's strength and stability. Laying patterns include *stretcher bond* where the bricks are laid lengthways and which is good for single-leaf walls; *English bond* which lays down alternately stretchers (lengthways) and headers (end-on); *Flemish bond* where a mixture of stretchers and headers are alternated at each course (layer); *English garden wall bond* which features two or more courses of stretchers to one of headers; and *Flemish wall bond* with one header and three stretchers to each course.

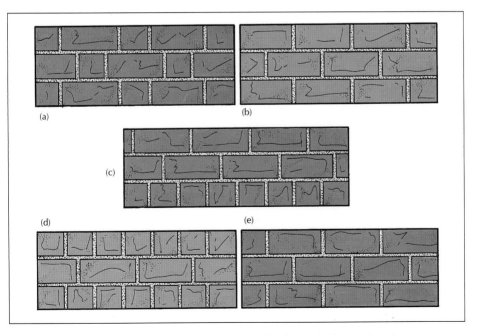

Bricks can be laid in a variety of patterns or bonds which will influence both strength and appearance: (a) stretcher bond, bricks laid lengthways, good for single-skin walls; (b) English bond, alternate courses of stretchers and headers; (c) English garden wall bond, two or more courses of stretchers to one of headers; (d) Flemish wall bond, one header and three stretchers on each course; (e) Flemish bond, alternate stretchers and headers on each course.

Bricklaying itself is not difficult but it would be advisable to practise on a smaller project, such as a patio wall or built-in barbecue, before tackling a major job such as a boundary wall. A long boundary wall will require strengthening piers about every 2.5m (8ft). Good foundations are essential for walls: they need to be about three times deeper than the width of the wall, although with a low wall this can be reduced to twice the width. First dig a trench to the appropriate depth: the top of the finished foundations should be several inches below ground level. Put down a layer of hardcore, and then concrete which is tamped down to compact it and left for a week to harden. Single-skin walls (one brick width) need 13cm (5in) of hardcore and 15cm (6in) of concrete made with one part cement to five parts combined aggregate; a double-skin wall (two bricks' width) should have a 23cm (9in) thickness of concrete and 13cm (5in) of hardcore.

To lay the first course of bricks which lies partially below ground level, make a strong mortar mix of one part masonry cement to three parts sharp sand. For the following courses, the mix should be adjusted to one part masonry cement to four or five parts soft sand. The usual procedure is to build up the corners, then fill in the gaps between them. This helps to keep the wall straight. To lay a brick, you place a blob of mortar on the centre of the brick and roll it with a cement trowel until it covers the surface in a smooth layer about 1cm (½in) thick; where the brick is going to be placed between two others, you will need a dab of mortar at each end too. The brick should be pressed into place, then tapped level with the handle of the trowel. Scrape away any excess mortar that escapes from the joins with the trowel for a neat finish.

For paths and paving, bricks are usually loose-laid on a bed of sand. For an intricate herring-bone or weave design, it is best to work the pattern out on paper first.

Stone

Natural stone immediately makes paths and patios look as though they have been in place for years, but this can be one of the most expensive garden materials, especially considering that some of the better concrete imitation pavers are quite convincing. You

Cotton lavender (*Santolina chamae-cyparissus*) is a fabulous companion for hard landscaping features. Available in grey or green (*Sempervirens*), its feathery aromatic foliage can be clipped into domes or formal hedging alongside paths or in patio beds. It would make a good feature either side of the entrance through a patio wall or, given its preference for a sunny situation and a light soil, could be grown along the top of a stone wall feature. If left unclipped, *Santolina* produces a mass of tiny pom-pom yellow flowers on slender stems.

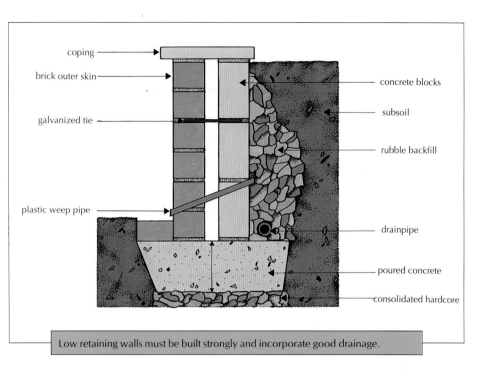

coping

brick outer skin

galvanized tie

plastic weep pipe

concrete blocks

subsoil

rubble backfill

drainpipe

poured concrete

consolidated hardcore

Low retaining walls must be built strongly and incorporate good drainage.

will find that the stone is usually sandstone or limestone, sold in regular slabs or 13–25sq cm (5–10sq in) pavement setts for paving, in broken pieces for crazy paving areas, dressed blocks for wall building, and 'random stone' which is the type usually used for walls. For stability, a random stone wall needs to be wide for its height and so is rarely taller than around 90cm (3ft). It must have good concrete foundations (as described above) and you should use the larger stones at the bottom, layering the smaller ones towards the top to create a slightly tapered effect. Save some of the larger stones to place horizontally across the wall as ties. If you are relatively inexperienced, it is probably best to mortar the stones in position using a one part cement to five parts sharp sand mix; when you feel more confident, you might like to attempt a drystone wall which looks especially effective in an informal garden.

Drystone walls take practice to build correctly, but have a wonderfully natural feel especially when planted with rock-loving plants to soften the effect of the stone.

Crazy paving gives an informal charm to paths and paved areas.

A herb wheel makes a lovely feature within a grass or gravel area and is very easy to construct.

Stone slabs or setts used for paving can be laid in the same way as concrete pavers and look good when mixed with complementary materials that can offer contrasting textures such as cobbles, gravel, pebbles and sand. Round cobbles are usually positioned at random in a bed of concrete, but you can buy square cobble setts which are as easy to lay as paving slabs.

Timber

Timber is so versatile that it can be used throughout the garden in many different guises, to create a decked area, fences, pergolas, arches, screens, even seats and plant containers. It can be rough-finished or smooth, specially treated so that it needs no maintenance, varnished, stained or even painted.

Fences

When planning a fence, you may need close-boarding for privacy; if privacy is less of a problem, an open ranch-style fence is only one option in a wide range of designs that include decorative wavy patterns along the top and keyhole 'windows' to allow for a fine view. You might prefer post-and-rail style fencing, which has the disadvantage that it is not animal-proof and is usually painted white so brings with it a regular maintenance commitment. For screening within the garden plan, less substantial but more decorative options include trellis panels, erected the same way as fence panels, bamboo or reed screens, and wattle or willow hurdles.

A solid fence is only as strong as its posts and, since it will have to take a considerable amount of wind resistance, these have to be as stable as you can make them.

Trellis can be erected and used to train climbers or cordon and espalier trees which, once established, will make attractive screening.

Actinidia kolomikta is a lovely twining climber whose woody stems are completely masked by a curtain of large, strongly marked leaves. The deciduous foliage produces a dappled effect of bright green, creamy-white and pink, which is ideal for walls and trellis. It produces small, cup-shaped white flowers in summer, male and female being borne on separate plants. Unlike most Actinidias which prefer partial shade, *A. kolomikta* will actually tolerate full sun. It prefers a well-drained but not too dry soil.

Timber posts come in different sizes and you should allow for a good depth to be in the ground: at least 30cm (1ft) for a fence 60cm (2ft) high; a minimum of 75cm (2ft 6in) for a fence 180cm (6ft) high. Timber posts should be well impregnated with preservative or pressure-treated to prevent them from rotting. Instead of cementing the posts into the ground, you can insert them into metal-spiked supports which you drive into the ground with a sledge-hammer. These protect the post from rotting, but it can be difficult to get them straight in stony or hard ground. Concrete posts are the most practical option; these can be purchased with a groove specially designed to take a fencing panel. Never try to erect a fence on a windy day.

Erecting a wooden fence is really a two-person job, so get some help if you can. Begin by marking the line where the fence will go with two stakes and a length of string or twine stretched between. Lay out all the posts on the ground approximately where they will go, remembering that the distance between the centre of one post and the next is not equal to the length of the fencing panel, but of the panel plus the post. Dig the first hole to the correct size and depth using a spade, or a post-hole borer if the fence is a long one. Put bricks or rubble in the bottom of the hole to keep the post upright while you check it is straight in all directions using a long spirit-level. When you have it right, pack more rubble around the base of the post and check again.

Lay the first panel out on the ground, butting it up against the post to judge the position of the next one. Dig out the next hole and insert the post, checking the verticals as before. You should also check that it is the same height as your first post by using a string stretched taut between the two, or by using a spirit-level on a plank across the tops. Where a fence has rails that have to be jointed to the post, the rails should be fitted into the first post before you put the second in position. Fix the panel into position using galvanized nails or screws. Continue with the next post and panel and so on until the fence is completed, using a line stretched between the end posts to make sure the height of the top of the fence is even. You can firm in the posts with compacted soil, but concreting them in is better. Temporary struts nailed to the posts will keep them vertical until the concrete has set.

Arches and Pergolas

To add height and useful support for climbing plants, timber is ideal for building arches, walkways and pergolas. For a rustic look, use peeled larch or chestnut poles which are simply notched and fixed together. Alternatively, 10 × 5cm (4 × 2in) planed wood can make an attractively arched tunnel, or build a cross-piece framework with 15 × 5cm (6 × 2in) sawn boards — overlapping the boards slightly at the ends looks more attractive, especially if they are sawn at an angle. If you are using the pergola as a walkway, not just as an overhead plant support for a patio or paved area, it should be at least 2m (6ft) wide.

Timber walkways blend well with other features and can be used to cross grass, water, planting beds or, as here, a rocky dry stream in a scheme with an oriental atmosphere.

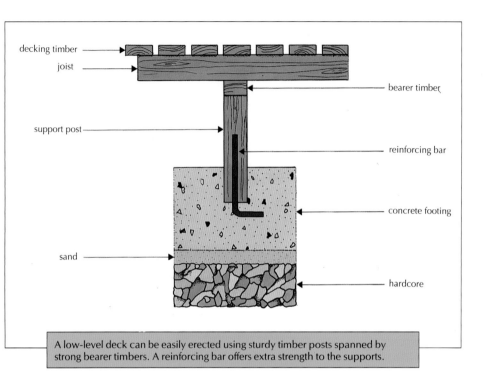

decking timber
joist
support post
sand

bearer timber
reinforcing bar
concrete footing
hardcore

A low-level deck can be easily erected using sturdy timber posts spanned by strong bearer timbers. A reinforcing bar offers extra strength to the supports.

Timber-Decking

Timber-decking is a smart and very versatile paving surface that can be adapted to any shape or size. Low-level decking that is no higher than 1m (3ft) off the ground, is simple to construct. Higher decking or changes in level may need professional advice. The decking can be laid in zigzag patterns or weave designs, in the same way as brick, for a more decorative finish, and varnished, stained or painted in a wide choice of natural and coloured effects. Specially treated posts or metal fencing spikes are necessary for support. The posts should be 10 × 10cm (4 × 4in) or 15 × 15cm (6 × 6in) depending on how far apart you intend to space them. They should not be any more than 1.8m (6ft) apart. The horizontal joists or

bearing timbers should be 7.5 × 10cm (3 × 4in) and positioned about 1–1.2m (3–4ft) apart. This will allow the timbers to overhang the bearers by about 7.5cm (3in) for a neater finish. Choose 2.5 × 5cm (1 × 2in), 2.5 × 7.5cm (1 × 3in) or 2.5 × 10cm (1 × 4in) timber for the surface; a slightly bevelled edge gives a finer finish. All fixing screws and nails should be galvanized and the screw heads countersunk for a neater finish. Remember that if you have chosen a more decorative design, the timber will have to be nailed every time it changes direction. Higher decks should be fitted with a handrail. This can be made quite easily by extending the support posts and attaching a horizontal rail made from rounded timber with a diameter of about 7.5cm (3in), or a piece of bamboo or ship's rope.

3 • PATIOS AND PAVED AREAS

A patio is usually a priority feature and whether paved, brick, concrete·or timber-decking, is essentially a firm, dry, level area used as a kind of outdoor living space complete with comfortable furniture for lounging, tables and chairs, and possibly even cooking facilities in the form of a barbecue. Although it makes a useful link between house and garden, a patio should be positioned where it will receive maximum sunshine and if this means the opposite end of the garden some kind of dry access from the house, such as a path or stepping-stones, is important. Sometimes it makes sense to position the patio in front of a summer-house or beside a swimming-pool rather than close to the house. If your garden is large enough, more than one patio area is the ideal, maybe in different styles and equipped to meet your varying needs.

In many ways the patio will be the starting point for the majority of other hard landscaping features in the garden. Some form of protection will almost definitely be required, especially if the area does not enjoy the protection of being close to the house wall. You will want the area to be private, shielded from the attention of neighbours and free from draughts if it is to be comfortable to use. Sometimes you will also need screening from the very sunshine the patio was built to catch, and some kind of overhead screening such as an awning attached to the side of the house, a large umbrella or a pergola structure shaded by

Raised beds incorporated into your patio design help to break up large areas of paving. Here the soil has been dug out to a depth of about 30cm (12in) and a paving slab placed in position against the paved surface, checking that it is upright and level. Hardcore is piled behind it to hold it in place. When all the slabs are in position, the layer of hardcore is built up to 30cm (12in) and then topped with a layer of gravel or pebbles before filling with compost.

bamboo screens or climbing plants will have to be considered.

There is also the possibility of an integrated water feature on the patio; if not a raised pool, then perhaps a small moving water feature, such as a wall-mounted spout or a small bubble fountain, which takes up very little room and is easy to install. Such a feature could be used to create a focal point and relaxing element to your patio. You will also want to furnish the area with built-in or free-standing seating suited to your style and budget and, to finish the whole thing off, organize raised beds or tubs and containers to hold your choice of patio plants.

All these elements must be planned as an integral part of the patio, just as the patio itself should be blended into the general garden scheme. This may be simply by

A co-ordinated range of bricks and pavers have been used to create a fully integrated patio area complete with raised beds, useful for off-setting such a large area of hard landscaping.

Simple flagstones edged with lavender conjure up an old-fashioned country cottage atmosphere.

means of its position within the plot or through a linking device such as a low wall or set of steps. Sometimes the patio is on a different level to the rest of the garden and serves as a kind of stage from which to view softer landscaping features.

Surface and Style

Your chosen paving surface will directly influence the look and style of your patio and affect its performance too. Concrete is inexpensive and versatile in that it can easily be laid to fit any shape, but it can appear a little bland over large areas. You can make it look more interesting by adding colours, chippings or paving patterns as described in Chapter 2, or you can mix materials, with areas of pebbles, brick or tile to add interest. You might prefer to buy preformed concrete paving slabs which are certainly easier for the amateur to handle. These are available in a wide range of shapes and finishes including imitation stone and brick, so almost anything is possible, from country-style flagstones to a smartly formal area combining interlocking shapes and different colours in a geometric design. If you are planning an intricate design or a mixture of paving effects, it is important to plan it out carefully first on paper so that you order the correct number of components. Mistakes can be expensive. With any paving material, if your design can utilize as many complete units as possible it will reduce wastage and save you time cutting and fitting difficult pieces.

You can buy natural stone paving slabs or setts which give an instantly mature look, but these are expensive. The secret is to use them sparingly while achieving the same kind of look and feel. If you cannot afford enough stone for a path, have stepping-stones instead and halve your paving order. Over a large patio area, mix the slabs with complementary materials such as gravel, old brick or areas of creeping herbs. Brick is versatile enough to create a cottage atmosphere, a Mediterranean style patio or a formal city look, depending on the type of brick you use and the way they are laid. They must be a type recommended for paving use to ensure that they can withstand the weathering, but that still leaves plenty of choice of colours and finishes from the traditional russets and browns to black, blue and yellow. You could create bands or borders in contrasting colours, or use the shape of the bricks themselves to devise intricate weave patterns. Outdoor quality quarry tiles can be used in the same way to create a distinctive Continental feel and are available in a similar range of shades. Frost-free patios might even consider floor-grade ceramic tiles or a mosaic design, maybe set into an area of other materials.

For a very different effect, timber makes an excellent patio surface where the planks are fitted to create a continuous decked area. This can be adjusted to any size or shape and is an excellent way to cope with

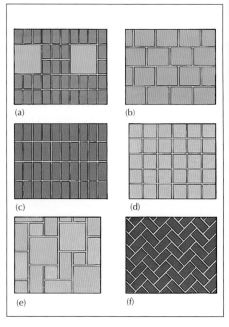

(a)　　　　　(b)

(c)　　　　　(d)

(e)　　　　　(f)

Paving slabs, stone and brick can be laid in an infinite variety of patterns. (a) Mixing concrete slabs with bricks. (b) Staggering the joints when laying plain paving slabs makes them look more interesting. (c) Mediterranean terracotta tiles. (d) Square concrete pavers. (e) Different sizes, shapes and colours produce a crazy paving effect. (f) Bricks or blocks laid in a herring-bone pattern.

a difficult patch of terrain or a change of level without the expensive and tedious levelling and backfilling other paving materials would require. The decking can be only a few centimetres off the ground or considerably higher, raised by means of wooden posts and joists. Where the deck is to adjoin the house, it can be fastened to the wall using coach bolts. If you want to make the area more decorative, the timber can be laid in weave patterns like brick, or stained and painted in soft earthy colours. You can use either softwoods or hardwoods to make decking. Western red cedar and chestnut are popular as they are easy to maintain and slow to rot; softwoods like deal and pine are more prone to splitting and will have to be treated with preservative once a year.

With any of these paving materials, timber-decking included, it is worth leaving some sections in your plan free to be used as planting areas. This is not only an attractive way to break up the surface, it introduces a softening, colourful element and also saves you money on materials.

Preparation

Your choice of paving material will create a definite look and atmosphere on the patio that will influence your whole garden plan. However, its true success relies on good planning, thorough preparation of the area and careful construction. Before you start your design, you should draw up an accurate scale plan of the area on graph paper, marking in any permanent fixtures such as man-hole covers, water-pipes or possibly trees that will have to be worked around. If you use squared paper, you could take each square to represent a single unit of your chosen paving material and this will make it simpler to plan and calculate the materials you need to order. Use different colours to plot in a more detailed design if you intend to use a mixture of unit types. At the same time mark in to scale any patio features you want to include, such as a pool, planting areas or built-in furniture. If you are not confident working on paper alone, go out into the garden and sketch out your ideas on the ground using pegs and string or a hosepipe for curves, so that an approximation of the design can be viewed from different angles around the garden. Looking down on your plan from a upstairs window can be a useful perspective.

When you are happy with the design you have created, you can order your materials

An informal patio relies on natural stone effect slabs, plenty of foliage and flowering plants to blur the edges.

and start preparing the site. Make sure you have all the tools and materials you need before starting work and do not attempt to lay concrete or paving if there is any chance of frost. You should begin by marking out the area using pegs and string strictly according to your plan. Use a spirit-level and a straight-edge to check each peg and ensure the layout is level. It is advisable always to work from a single reference peg – called a datum peg – not from peg to peg,

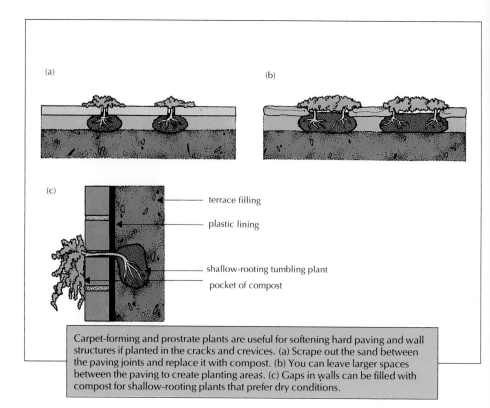

(a)

(b)

(c)

terrace filling

plastic lining

shallow-rooting tumbling plant

pocket of compost

Carpet-forming and prostrate plants are useful for softening hard paving and wall structures if planted in the cracks and crevices. (a) Scrape out the sand between the paving joints and replace it with compost. (b) You can leave larger spaces between the paving to create planting areas. (c) Gaps in walls can be filled with compost for shallow-rooting plants that prefer dry conditions.

to avoid errors creeping in. The pegs will have to be adjusted to allow for a slight fall towards the house to prevent standing rainwater. For example, a patio about 3m (10ft) broad will need a fall of about 1 in 100. Before you start excavating, check that the finished level, taking into account your footings and the thickness of the paving, will not be less than 15cm (6in) below the damp-proof course of any adjoining building. If the course is near the ground, you will have to insert on its edge a plank about 2cm (⅞in) thick on the footings after excavation in order to leave a 2.5cm (1in) gutter. This will enable any debris likely to breach the damp-proof course to be cleaned out regularly.

Begin excavations by removing all the topsoil and storing this separately as it can be used for patio planting beds or elsewhere in the garden. The area should be left roughly level. It is possible for slabs and bricks to be loose-laid on an 8cm (3¼in) bed of sand, but other unit paving materials and concrete require a 7.5cm (3in) layer of hardcore such as broken stones, brick and rubble, which must be tamped down as level as possible on to the excavated soil. A heavy-duty roller or special vibrating machine is the best tool for the job and can be hired from your local tool hire shop. You must top the hardcore with a blinding layer of sand or sand and cement to a depth of about 2.5cm (1in). This in turn must be raked and the surface rolled again to make it level.

4 • WALLS AND FENCES

Defining the boundaries of your plot will probably be your first task when it comes to choosing and budgeting for garden features. Unless they are at the point of collapse, the walls and fences that run around your garden tend to be ignored, but they do make an important and dominant contribution to the look of your overall scheme. They need not be dull, for the options are wide according to your needs. Before you do anything, you should check exactly which boundaries you are responsible for, as the cost may be shared with a neighbour. Where existing boundaries are not to your taste and you cannot afford to change them, or they are your neighbour's choice, you can always disguise them in some way to make them more in keeping with your garden design. This might involve the erection of trellis to support a curtain of foliage or flowering climbing plants, or simply a series of bamboo or reed screens in front of the offending item.

Walls, fences and screens can be used to serve two distinct roles within the garden – to provide privacy or screening – and their purpose will dictate your choice to a large extent. If you need something substantial for privacy or shelter, there is no point in buying the cheaper kind of fencing like woven larch panels because they cannot stand up to strong winds and once damaged will need replacing. For privacy you need something like close-boarded fencing or a brick wall, but these are not good at withstanding really strong winds as they offer too much resistance. The wind tends to travel over the top creating nasty draughts in the garden. Better in this situation is a lattice-type fence or even a hedge which tends to filter the draughts and reduce their strength. Hedges take longer to establish than fences or walls, but you can always put up a temporary fencing effect such as chestnut palings to keep animals and intruders out until the plants have matured. Hedges will need a little care and regular

Walls can be brightened up in summer by using baskets of colourful annuals suspended from strong brackets.

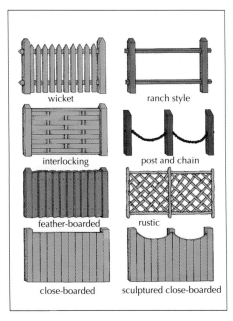

wicket   ranch style

interlocking   post and chain

feather-boarded   rustic

close-boarded   sculptured close-boarded

Different types of timber fencing can be selected to suit a particular location.

vines trailed along fence
and tied to the rail at intervals

training wire stapled to posts

Self-supporting plants will cling to most types of fencing, but most climbers need some assistance in the form of wires or ties.

trimming in the growing season, but their natural leafy appearance might justify the extra work. To grow a hedge from scratch, suitable shrubs such as holly, quickthorn (hawthorn), blackthorn, beech and yew, should be planted about 50–100cm (18–36in) apart. For quick results you may prefer an evergreen conifer, like Lawson's cypress which can be trained to any height.

For screening off areas within your garden plan you can make use of more ornamental but less sturdy features such as screens and panels or low walls. These are available in a wide range of styles and can be used to disguise an eyesore such as the dustbins or a parked caravan, to screen off a separate part of the garden like the vegetable plot, or to create new areas or 'rooms' within the main scheme. Bamboo and reed screens make a wonderfully natural backdrop for plants or can be used to screen a patio area. They look particularly good if you are hoping to create an oriental atmosphere in part of the garden. These screens are not particularly durable, however, and you should expect to replace them within four to five years. Also available are trellis panels, which can be used as screening where you want cover from climbing plants, and wattle or willow hurdles. The hurdles are supported by stakes driven into the ground and because these tend to rot, the lifespan of this feature will be between five and ten years.

Walls

Walls are the most expensive form of

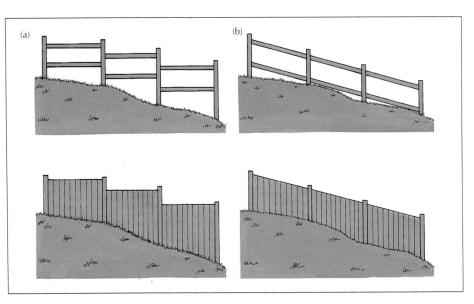

Fencing a sloping site. (a) Insert the main fencing posts 2m (6ft) apart, then screw the cross-struts into position using a spirit-level to get them straight. The fencing panels can then be fixed to the frame. (b) Where the fence follows the general slope of the ground, the highest and lowest posts are positioned first; then the depth to which the others are to be sunk is determined by stretching a piece of string from the top of one post to the other.

boundary feature, both in terms of money and time spent erecting them. However, built well, they are long-lasting, effective and can be very attractive too. If you are committed to a long expanse of wall, any unrelieved stretch of one material can look rather overpowering so you might consider mixing materials: adding an area of stone into a brick wall, for example, or including a section of ornamental pierced patio blocks into a block wall. Alternatively you could use different colours and shapes to create a pattern or design within a brick or block wall.

On a practical level, size as well as style will have to be considered when planning walls. Length is more or less predetermined by your plot, but the height will need careful thought. There may be planning restrictions in your area on the height of walls, so do check first with your local planning officer. Also, height will affect the cost of the finished feature; for example, a 120cm (4ft) wall uses four times the number of bricks than one 60cm (2ft) high because

Warm red brick is probably the most attractive type of high boundary wall for informal or traditional gardens.

An ornamental spout mounted on the wall and pouring water into a pool or basin makes a delightful feature, but you should make sure bricks are suitably waterproofed.

it needs a double thickness of bricks for stability.

Brick walls are the most common in gardens and for a taller wall this is definitely the most practical option. Bricks can also be used successfully to build low single-skin boundary walls no more than 45cm (18in) high, which are useful at the front of the house or bordering a patio. A brick wall any taller than this should be double-skin and depending on the bond pattern you choose (*see* Chapter 2) you may have to cut a lot of bricks in order to fit the design, which can be expensive. Tall, long walls may need expansion joints; it is advisable to consult a professional or a more detailed manual if you have not done much bricklaying before. It is important to buy only frost-resistant bricks, not house bricks which cannot withstand the weather conditions in an exposed situation. Also, do not forget that bricks vary in finish as well as colour, some being quite rough for rustic effects, others smoother and smarter for formal gardens.

Natural stone makes a delightful walling material: it soon weathers and will even support plant material, mosses and lichens. A stone wall looks particularly appropriate in a traditional or country style garden. However, stone is expensive to buy so unless you have a ready source of random stone nearby or on-site you may be limited to a small wall, designed mainly as a decorative feature. For the beginner, mortaring the stones is probably a good idea, but with practice you might enjoy tackling a drystone wall.

Also available for garden walls are concrete walling blocks which, because they

You can stand ornamental urns and pots on top of low walls as an additional feature.

For building a drystone wall, use rocks 5–20cm (2–8in) thick. Build up the wall, placing the rocks so that they tilt slightly backwards, with the stone below.

are regularly shaped, are easy to lay. They come in a wide range of colours and finishes, including imitation stone at a fraction of the cost of the real thing; some imitations are better than others. The blocks are laid in the same way as bricks. More ornamental and usually used to build patio walls are pierced or screen concrete blocks. These might be square, rectangular or even circular, with a variety of holey designs to choose from. Being pierced, they make a

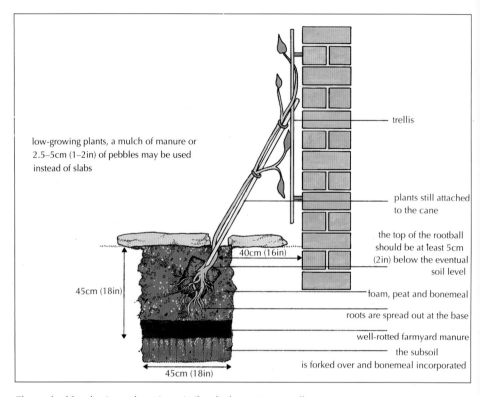

low-growing plants, a mulch of manure or 2.5–5cm (1–2in) of pebbles may be used instead of slabs

trellis

plants still attached to the cane

the top of the rootball should be at least 5cm (2in) below the eventual soil level

40cm (16in)

45cm (18in)

loam, peat and bonemeal

roots are spread out at the base

well-rotted farmyard manure

the subsoil is forked over and bonemeal incorporated

45cm (18in)

The method for planting a clematis or similar climber against a wall.

good wind barrier and because the blocks tend to be large they are quick and easy to lay. They can be used within the boundary wall if used as a decorative feature.

Fences

The quickest way to screen off your garden is to erect a fence. Timber is the softest and most natural choice of material, although it can look a little raw until the colour has weathered. However, fencing can also be made from wire, chain-link or concrete slabs if appearance is of less importance. For total privacy you need a close-boarded type of fence which is supplied in panels to

be fixed to strong concrete or timber posts. If you simply want to indicate the boundaries of your plot and the general style is open plan, a ranch-style fence where horizontal bars are fixed between posts is a practical option. You can buy this kind of fencing in kit form with horizontal planks approximately 10–15cm (4–6in) wide and 2.5cm (1in) thick. These are spaced at 10cm (4in) intervals and are designed to fix to PVC posts; in fact, you can purchase the whole fence in PVC if you do not fancy the burden of painting it every year, as this style of fence is often painted white.

A wire fence is not particularly attractive but where you do not need the privacy of bricks or close-boarding, or if you wish to make use of a distant view, it can be surprisingly unobtrusive, especially if you plant shrubs along its length. It is also strong and inexpensive, although plastic-coated wire mesh is more durable than galvanized wire and is more suitable for gardens. Chain-link fences are quick and easy to erect, being attached to regularly spaced posts made of angle iron (although concrete or wooden posts may be used), and are simply tightened to achieve the correct tension. Strength and stability will be aided if you brace the end posts with angled struts, ideally concreted into the ground in the same way as the posts. Wires are usually fixed at the top and bottom to keep the mesh in place. These are fixed to the winders bolted to the angle iron at the end and corner posts. Fences higher than 1.2m (4ft) should be fitted with three wires, at the top, middle and bottom, to keep the

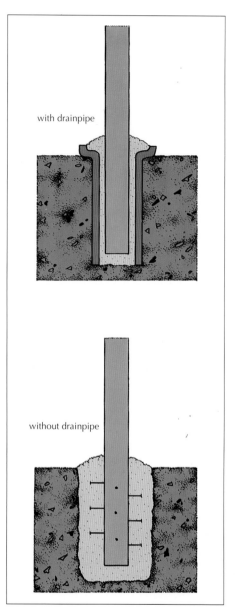

with drainpipe

without drainpipe

Fence posts must be well anchored in the soil to give adequate support. If you use concrete, the post must be supported until the concrete has set.

A plant which can offer both attractive leaves and foliage all summer is a real asset for patio containers. These free-flowering ivy-leaved geraniums (pelargoniums) have been fastened to a wall-mounted trellis, but would look equally good cascading out of a tub or hanging basket. The pretty lobed leaves are similar to those of zonal pelargoniums, and given a warm, sunny, sheltered position will produce a mass of delicate pink flowers until the first frosts. All the bedding geraniums can be relied on to produce a long and colourful show of blooms so long as they get plenty of sunshine.

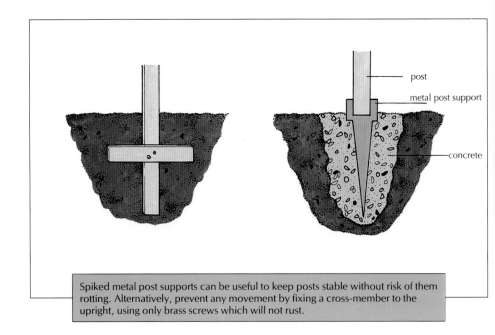

Spiked metal post supports can be useful to keep posts stable without risk of them rotting. Alternatively, prevent any movement by fixing a cross-member to the upright, using only brass screws which will not rust.

mesh taut. The wires are fastened to the mesh every 15cm (6in) along the top wire and every 45cm (18in) along the others.
. To erect a chain-link fence, you must begin by marking out where you want it to go with string. The posts should be inserted

Even the plainest stretch of fencing can be transformed by an old table and a collection of sweet-scented plants.

no more than 3m (10ft) apart into level ground and concreted into position. The holes for the posts should be approximately 45cm (18in) square and 60cm (2ft) deep for a fence about 120cm (4ft) high. Taller fences will require a depth nearer 75cm (30in). You will also need straining holes about 45 × 30cm (18 × 12in) and 45cm (18in) deep. Make sure these are on the right side of the fence to take the strain. Once the posts are in position, you can unroll the wire and strain it between the posts, passing a stretcher bar through the last row of mesh and bolting it to the post. You will have to use screwed eye-bolts if tensioning wire between concrete or timber posts. As you unroll the wire, you should try to keep it taut, fixing it temporarily to the line wires with plant ties. Maintain tension as you fasten the mesh to each intermediate and straining post. When the fence is completed you can fix the mesh to the line wires with tying wire.

5 • PATHS, STEPS AND BRIDGES

You need safe, dry, all-weather access to features around the garden, but the role of paths, bridges and walkways is not purely a practical one. They need to look good too and, importantly, to fit well within your overall garden scheme. You can even use such features as a design tool. A path or stepping-stones may lead the eye into the distance to create a vista, or describe a winding route that disguises the true boundaries of the plot. A series of steps or a bridge, even if small, suggest adventure and excitement, a sense of stepping into new territories. Attractively constructed, their role can easily become that of a focal point within a smaller garden.

Paths

A straight path which takes you directly

Formal paths have their place in layouts like this where concrete paths divide the garden into neatly planted areas and provide safe, dry access around the plot.

A short flight of steps leading down to a patio on the next level has been blended well with the rest of the garden by using pots and tubs of plants.

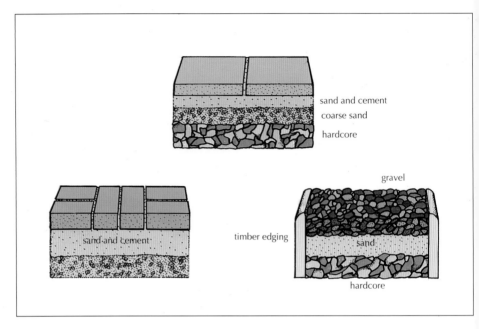

sand and cement
coarse sand
hardcore

gravel

sand and cement

timber edging

sand

hardcore

Hard-surface paths must be laid on a level, well-drained base. Remove the topsoil, then make sure the sub-soil is well compacted before putting down a layer of coarse sand or hardcore topped with coarse sand. Next, bed bricks or slabs into a sand and cement mix (1 part cement to 4 of sand). To finish off, brush more sand and cement between them and spray with water to set the cement. Gravel paths need a retaining kerbstone or timber edging. If brick or paving stone paths are similarly edged, this should be put in first.

from A to B only has its place in the strictly formal garden where a network of paths in turf, gravel or concrete creates the geometric framework within which the other features are planned. Generally, paths are more enjoyable both visually and physically where they take a more circuitous route through the garden. This can not only help disguise the true dimensions of the site by disappearing from view behind screens and shrubs, but will also encourage a more leisurely walking pace, suggesting the garden is bigger than it really is. The only exception is in larger gardens where you are trying to achieve the effect of an avenue. Long, straight and uncompromising, an avenue leads the eye directly to a distant vista –

which might possibly be little more than an attractive bench seat – and is formally bordered by trees or shrubs: pleached lime trees perhaps, or standard roses, lavender bushes, clipped yew shapes or even a low formal hedge in box or yew.

A covered walkway can be attractive even in a small garden: a wide path can be completely overhung by a pergola or hooped structure smothered in climbing plants such as vines, roses or wisteria so that the blooms hang down to create a kind of tunnel. This effect can also be achieved without the aid of a major structure by training fruit trees, usually apple, across wires until they meet to form a continuous archway.

Sometimes a path is a useful device to divide the lawn from the border as it makes mowing easier and plants can be allowed to spill over the edges. In this case, the shape and direction of your path will be dictated by that of your planting beds. Even where the path is an important element in the basic design of the garden, you do not want it to appear too dominant so try not to position it in full sun where it will catch the eye – save these good growing areas for your plants.

Whatever their visual appeal, it is important that paths work well on a practical level too. They should provide useful access to various parts of the garden, particularly in bad weather, and the surface must be level and non-slippery. There is a wide range of styles and materials to choose from depending on the overall look of the rest of the garden. It makes good design sense to take your lead from other hard landscaping features and keep your paths in style by using the same or similar materials; you could save money too if it gives you the chance to utilize materials left over from building a patio or wall. Sometimes a certain type of path just seems perfect for your kind of garden: a winding patchwork of bricks around the country cottage; smart paviors linking features in a small but perfectly arranged city back yard. In a large garden a combination of materials might be more interesting: a formal style to run beside the herbaceous borders; grass or bark chips running through the shrubbery. In any garden plot, experimenting with an abrupt change of materials along the length of a winding path might produce an interesting and exciting result. All paths benefit from allowing nearby plants to creep over the edges a little and soften the outline. Where you are using pavers, you can even plan for low-growing creepers to grow between the slabs.

Concrete is practical but not particularly exciting unless you use a pattern stamp or

Rosa rugosa, sometimes called the hedgehog Rose or Japanese rose, makes a grand sprawl of attractive bright green leaves and large single white or reddish-purple cup-shaped open blooms. It will grow as broad as it is tall, around 1–2m (3–6ft). The flowers are scented and in autumn are followed by large, striking hips for additional autumn interest. *Rosa rugosa*'s informal appearance and the fact that it flowers consistently right through the summer into autumn, makes this a good choice to soften more formal features such as brick or stone.

allow plants to smother the edges. It is a good option for vegetable plots and other, more formal areas of the garden, or to run along the side of the house, a shed or similar outbuilding. You will need to excavate the whole area and erect wooden shuttering to provide a framework into which the wet concrete is poured. Sprinkling the surface with gravel or shingle after smoothing will provide a rougher, non-slip surface and add a little texture too. More decorative are concrete paving slabs: square or oblong types look best in a formal setting and you might mix shapes and designs for extra interest.

Natural stone can be expensive for that well-established country cottage look, but crazy paving is a good option for a softer,

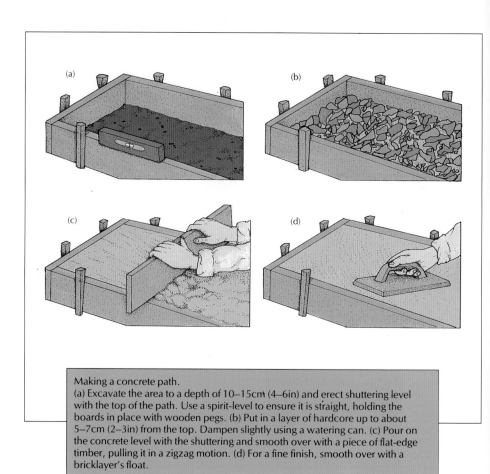

Making a concrete path.
(a) Excavate the area to a depth of 10–15cm (4–6in) and erect shuttering level with the top of the path. Use a spirit-level to ensure it is straight, holding the boards in place with wooden pegs. (b) Put in a layer of hardcore up to about 5–7cm (2–3in) from the top. Dampen slightly using a watering can. (c) Pour on the concrete level with the shuttering and smooth over with a piece of flat-edge timber, pulling it in a zigzag motion. (d) For a fine finish, smooth over with a bricklayer's float.

informal atmosphere. Brick can be loose-laid on sand and is adaptable to any style; use second-hand bricks or rough-textured types and lay in herring-bone or zigzag patterns for old-fashioned appeal.

Another less formal style of path but one that needs a little extra maintenance is wood or bark chips; this looks wonderfully natural in woodland areas. Alternatively use gravel or chippings for a more formal look. These materials are best used in conjunction with some kind of edging, such as treated timber boards or concrete kerbstones, to prevent them getting knocked over the rest of the garden.

Do not overlook the possibilities of grass as a path in certain areas: it may be wet and slippery in wet weather, but makes a fine route between formal herb or similar planting beds. Ideally the width of the path should equal that of your mower for easier maintenance; prepare yourself for all that edge cutting, too. You can buy a long-handled tool that makes the task less back-breaking; alternatively let plants spill over the edges and avoid the problem.

Stepping-Stones

Where a path may still seem too dominant within your garden scheme or if you find the costs of the materials required prohibitive, stepping-stones are an excellent alternative and have a certain charm all of their own. Again, a winding route seems to be the more attractive option, especially if the steps can disappear from view behind plants or screens. They can pick their way across grass, planting beds or water, wherever access is required. Paving slabs bedded into the soil or grass are an obvious choice, but you could also use bricks arranged in blocks of differing designs or buy patterned discs specially made for use as stepping-stones. Circular log slices also make ideal stepping-stones for informal or woodland areas, provided they are well treated against rot. Most important with any style of stepping-stone is to ensure that the distance between the steps is not too great, encouraging a slow, leisurely pace.

A change of level provides the opportunity to create a separate area within the main garden. These simple steps softened by flowers lead up to a seating area, then up again to another secluded area screened by shrubs and trees.

Stepping-stones wind their way through an interesting blend of flowering and foliage plants, obliterating any sense of this long narrow garden being boring.

Steps

A change of level in the garden or on the patio provides the perfect opportunity to install a series of steps. It is important that they are safely constructed without too large a stride between steps and with a level, non-slip surface. A step more than 30cm (1ft) high is considered uncomfortable for most people to negotiate. The tread of the step should be sloped slightly forward or to the sides to prevent standing rainwater. Where the steps are long and steep or where the garden is used by the elderly or people with a physical disability, a handrail is a practical addition. Ideally, each step should be about 45cm (18in) deep to

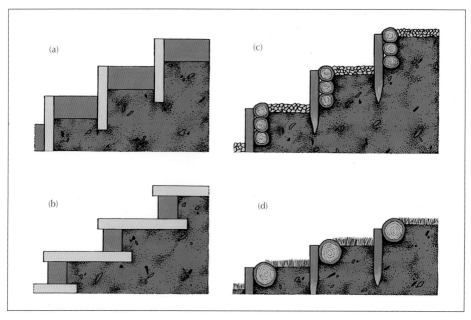

Steps can be designed to suit the style of your garden or patio: (a) informal timber steps using old railway sleepers; (b) a more formal look using paving slabs and bricks; (c) rustic logs held in place with wooden stakes; (d) shallow steps created using logs.

include a 5cm (2in) overlap, with a rise between each step of approximately 10cm (4in). You should normally start construction with the bottom step and work upwards, dividing the slope into the most practical number of steps.

Steps can also be visually important, accentuating a change of height or even becoming a decorative feature where positioned centrally and flanked by urns, ornaments or strong architectural plants. You often see steps leading down from the patio into the main part of the garden treated in this grand way. For a smart, strictly formal look, steps can be constructed in brick to include ornamental brickwork up the sides and maybe columns or pillars too at the top and bottom. Both brick and stone can be used to build a

curved flight of steps, which always looks particularly stylish. For more modest appeal mix brick risers with paving slabs, or design

An ornamental balustrade makes a fine feature flanking a flight of patio steps leading down into the garden.

Steps can be decorated with small pots and troughs of plants.

simple stone steps, perhaps climbing up beside an old stone wall smothered in trailing plants. The simplest type of step is made from timber, which might be planked or as basic as rustic logs held in place with wooden stakes as risers for a very informal, woodland feel.

Walkways and Bridges

Timber-planked walkways raised slightly above the ground can provide useful and visually exciting routes around the garden. They can be constructed in the same way as timber-decking (*see* Chapter 3) and incorporate all kinds of design possibilities such as weave designs or a change of direction to create various patterns. The sections themselves can be organized in many interesting ways, including zigzags and staggered staging with large plants at the intersections. They also cope easily with any changes of level without the need for steps. In this way you might use walkways as an extension of a timber-decked area or to span planting beds, lawn or water. The surface should be scrubbed or scored occasionally to prevent the build-up of slippery algae, and treated to a regular dose of preservative.

The curiously fleshy houseleek *Sempervivum* thrives in dry stony conditions making it the perfect hardy evergreen for growing on walls, banks and any rocky or stony feature. It prefers plenty of sun, in which conditions the plant will produce a tight carpet of attractive rosettes clinging to the stone by means of short stolons. *Sempervivum* can offer a whole range of variegated greens, reds, purples and pinks depending on type. Different varieties produce clusters of star-shaped flowers in summer, which might be anything from a greenish-red to yellowish-green with purple centres. The rosettes die off after the plant has flowered, but it self-generates simultaneously by means of tiny offsets which make this a very easy genus to propagate.

For crossing water, whether a small informal stream or a larger pond, a bridge provides access to new parts of the garden or an island area. This could be as simple as a log, a concrete slab or section of stone secured in concrete on either bank to provide

It is important that a bridge takes you somewhere, even if it is only to a small island area or another part of the garden. A simple timber bridge like this looks more impressive if you add handrails.

a low, natural-looking crossing place. Or you might long for something more elaborate and ornamental which can be used as the focal point of a major water feature. An elaborate concrete or stone bridge can be difficult and expensive to build and is usually beyond the scope of the average garden. Such structures are best left to the professionals. However, a single-span timber construction can be very effective and is relatively simple to build provided the span is no more than 2.4m (8ft). Beyond this point you will need additional support in the form of piers driven into the bed of the stream or pool. To span a large area of water, you might consider a Japanese style bridge which employs a series of overlapping timber-staging very like the walkways described above. You need 15 × 15cm (6 × 6in) support posts on either side about 15cm (6in) above the proposed level of the water. Onto these are bolted joists of 7.5 × 15cm (3 × 6in) timber to support wooden planks. Each section is arranged to overlap

the next and changes direction slightly to create a pleasing zigzag effect.

To construct a single-span timber bridge you will need to erect joist-supporting posts on both banks, making sure they are level by stretching a line between them and checking with a spirit-level. You can fasten 10 × 10cm (4 × 4in) timber joists to these to span the water and to support timber planking, nailed or screwed at right angles for stability. Planking can be 5 × 10cm (2 × 4in) or 5 × 15cm (2 × 6in) timber and should be secured with three 9cm (3½in) screws or 10cm (4in) nails. A handrail is a good idea for safety. This should be about 1m (3ft) high and firmly fixed, the top rail made from 5 × 5cm (2 × 2in) timber or 7.5cm (3in) diameter poles – not rustic poles which rot too quickly and might give the user splinters. All timber used near water should be well protected against rot with a suitable non-toxic preservative. You should check that any chemicals used are safe for fish and plants.

6 • PERGOLAS, TRELLIS AND ARCHES

The quickest way to add height to your garden plan is to erect a vertical structure: this might be a pergola, an arch or, for a real focal point in the centre of a lawn or patio, an ornamental gazebo which is like an open summer-house or band-stand. Such structures are mostly built in wood or metal but embrace a huge range of styles and sizes to choose from, so you are sure to find something to suit your garden. Although many are highly decorative, their primary purpose is to provide a support for climbing and trailing plants so most of the structure will be covered. You can have as much fun choosing plants as you do choosing the structure itself: interesting evergreen foliage like ivies; beautiful flowering climbers such as roses, clematis and wisteria; or the wonderful overhead scents of jasmine and honeysuckle.

As well as adding height, such features can have many other practical uses. They can be invaluable for casting a dappled shade over an area of the lawn or patio, or you can plan to use them as a focal point, to screen off other parts of the garden, or to create an entrance or walkway. Most are easily constructed, while certain styles can be purchased ready to erect.

Trellis is one of the most useful plant supports. You can make it yourself using a criss-cross of lathes or buy it in simple panels of squares or diagonal diamond shapes. It can be erected against an existing wall or fence to provide plant support, or installed as a free-standing screen by nailing it to wooden fence posts. There is also a more substantial style of trellis which is actually strong enough to be used as a boundary fence. This comes in a choice of ornamental styles and colours, and looks good enough to stand as a feature in its own right.

Pergolas

A pergola is really a kind of covered walkway

A decorative wrought-iron gate opens up a view through the arch in an old brick wall and makes the garden beyond seem secretive and special.

using a timber framework that can be as simple or elaborate as you choose. It is widely used as a means of shading the patio, but is also ideal to link the house to an outbuilding, such as a garage, across a side passage. If you want to use the pergola as a walkway, it must sensibly lead from one area to another and be at least 2m (6ft) wide. The simplest style of pergola is a wooden framework built using 10 × 5cm (4 × 2in) sawn

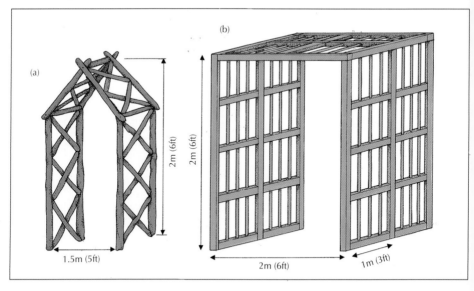

(a) A rustic archway constructed from larch or chestnut poles makes a delightful informal feature over a gate or entrance to another part of the garden, and can be used to support a climbing rose or honeysuckle.
(b) A pergola structure made from planed timber planks makes a substantial support for scented woody-stemmed climbers with pendulous blooms such as wisteria.

Pergolas can be constructed in whatever materials suit the style and scale of your patio; this simple arrangement of larch poles creates an unmistakably rustic appearance.

timber which is assembled to create a series of uprights joined in pairs. The resulting tunnel of arches can be linked across the top with cross-pieces. These look best protruding beyond the end of the structure and sawn at an angle to provide additional plant support for hanging baskets.

There is an infinite number of variations on the pergola theme. You can make a simple rustic structure for a country garden using peeled larch poles which only need notching and fitting together. Alternatively, the basic supports can be built like pillars in brick or stone with 15 × 5cm (6 × 2in) sawn boards used for the top structure.

The beauty of a pergola is that it can be used to grow a wide variety of climbing plants and, if well covered, can be relied on to filter light summer rain showers as well as strong sunlight. Alternatively, if you want to

Archways are simple structures to erect. They can be made from tubular steel, although timber or brick is usually more attractive until plants grow to cover the structure.

see some of the structure as an architectural part of your garden plan, allow only a couple of plants to grow to the top and use matting or screens when the sun is hot.

Arches

A decorative arch might be constructed from chestnut or larch poles for a rustic look, or be built from timber or, frequently, metal. It should be positioned where it creates a logical 'entrance' to the garden or at least part of the garden. It need not be set into a wall or length of fencing, but traditionally should be smothered in a flowering plant such as roses or honeysuckle. You might also organize a whole series of metal arches or hoops to create a continuous arched effect around an enclosed

area or to make a flower tunnel. You can buy a wide range of different wired components that can be fitted together to create all manner of elaborate arched effects and arbours.

Gazebos

Like a pergola, a gazebo provides a decorative place to sit in the shade and enjoy the colour, shape and scent of climbing plants. The structure is usually circular, for positioning on a small patio of its own or in the middle of the lawn where it makes a fine focal point. The style of gazebos tends to be ornate and most of the commercially produced gazebos are constructed in metal, but you can make your own simple version if you prefer by constructing a pointed roof

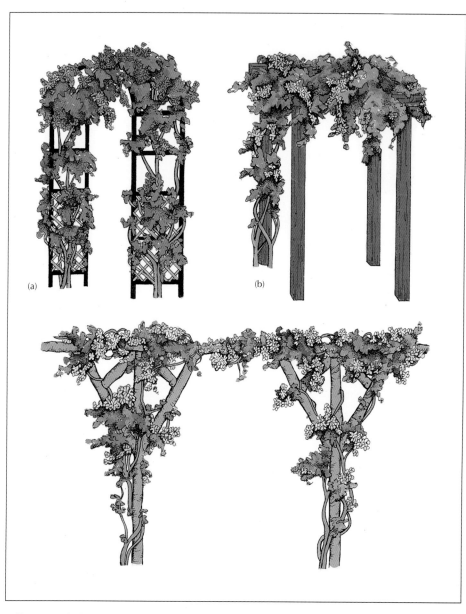

Tall-growing climbers that require hard pruning and produce a lot of blooms at the top are ideal for growing up supporting structures that need to be clothed well above ground level. (a) Simple metal or rustic arches. (b) Open rustic linked archways spanning the garden.

over a framework of timber or wrought-iron palings. Climbing plants can be trained to smother the supporting pillars or struts and even the roof.

Choosing Climbing Plants

Your choice of climbing plants to smother and soften your vertical features will depend on the effect you want to create. You will almost certainly want a few flowering climbers as they can look superb, making a hanging curtain of scent and colour over an arch or pergola during the summer months. Generally these plants prefer their foliage and flowers to bathe in full sun, but their roots to be in the shade so you may have to mulch the base of the plant with pebbles or woodchips.

For an informal country feature you cannot improve on the heady scent of honeysuckle or the mass of coloured blooms produced by a rambling rose. A more sophisticated display for formal gardens can be provided by wisteria's long scented racemes or the exotic passion flower (*Passiflora caerulea*) which may also produce strange fruits at the end of summer. Do not forget the potential of annual flowering climbers; these will quickly make good cover, yet die back for winter allowing valuable light to penetrate a pergola-covered patio, for example. The canary creeper (*Tropaeolum canariense*) will produce a mass of bright yellow flowers right through the summer. Popular nasturtiums (*Tropaeolum speciosum*) can also be relied on for a bright display; in this case, the brilliant flowers are red.

No garden is complete without at least one clematis, and some form of strong support is essential for this prolific group of flowering climbers. There are so many types to choose from that you are sure to find one, or two, which suit your own particular needs. *Clematis armandii*, for example, is an early flowering evergreen with the advantage that it will tolerate some shade; the *Montana* group are vigorous growers and will quickly smother a support, or roof, with small single flowers; there are large-bloomed cultivars which flower early in the season and produce lovely double or semi-double blooms; and clematis varieties that can enliven the patio or garden at the end of summer. Blooms vary from large flat-faced flowers to tubular or even bell-like types.

You will also want a few climbers valued for their attractive foliage to give balance and variety to your vertical display. Ivy is an obvious choice; another shade lover is *Parthenocissus henryana* which has lovely silvery white and pink variegated leaves with bright red autumn colour. For quick cover any of the following would be an excellent choice: Russian vine (*Polygonum baldschuanicum*) which will absolutely smother anything with a mass of fluffy white flowers in summer; the glory vine (*Vitis coignetiae*) which has the bonus of fruits and good autumn colour; the lovely climbing hydrangea (*Hydrangea petiolaris*); and the Persian ivy (*Hedera colchica*).

The position and use of your feature will determine whether you want to grow any evergreen climbers, they can be useful for winter interest in the garden, but over seating areas it is sometimes useful for more light to be allowed to penetrate during the shorter days. Some evergreens are almost too lovely to resist. In warmer climates or a well-sheltered site in the south or south-west you can grow tender but beautiful bougainvillea. *Abelia grandiflora* is another tender evergreen with lovely pink and white flowers right through the summer and into the autumn. Other more hardy evergreens include *Garrya eliptica* with its useful hanging catkins in winter, and the stunning Californian lilac (*Ceanothus thyrsiflorus*) which has blue flowers in summer.

7 • WATER FEATURES

A water feature is a real asset to any garden. For the small investment of time and money that it entails to install one, you will be rewarded by a wonderful visual lure, an excellent antidote to stress and, if correctly constructed, one of the most exciting and enjoyable areas of the garden in return for very little maintenance. Apart from the undeniable attraction of owning a pond, or the chance to observe a moving water feature such as a fountain or cascade in your own garden, one of the great things about water is its flexibility. It can be adapted to any size or style of plot from the largest country garden to the smallest city back yard or patio. Water can adopt any character from wildlife haven to sophisticated piece of moving water sculpture. You can spend a fortune or put together a fine feature on a shoe-string. There is simply no excuse for not having one.

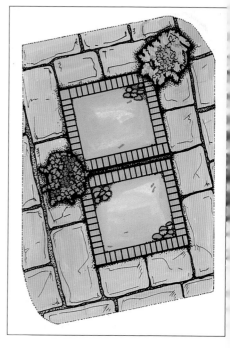

Two geometric pools edged in brick make an attractive patio feature with plants confined to pots for easy maintenance.

A bubble fountain provides an attractive small moving water feature that would suit virtually any size and style of garden or patio.

Pools and Ponds

If you can find the opportunity to install a pond, however small, you will never regret it. The reflecting qualities of the water add life and movement to a garden, as well as offering the chance to observe fish, wildlife and a fascinating variety of dramatic plants at close quarters. If digging a pool below ground is not practical, you can build one above ground; and if an informal swathe of water and lush plants is not really your style, a formal pool in all its geometric glory can be your choice.

It is worth taking the time and trouble to plan a pool correctly if you want to enjoy a relatively problem-free relationship. A sunny open position is important: too near to trees and you will have trouble with fallen leaves polluting the water. Also, the majority of water garden·plants require plenty of sunshine to flourish, particularly

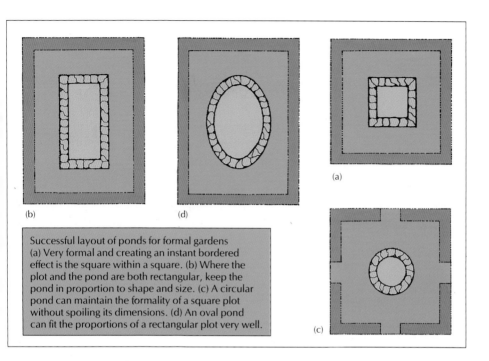

(a)

(b)   (d)

Successful layout of ponds for formal gardens
(a) Very formal and creating an instant bordered
effect is the square within a square. (b) Where the
plot and the pond are both rectangular, keep the
pond in proportion to shape and size. (c) A circular
pond can maintain the formality of a square plot
without spoiling its dimensions. (d) An oval pond
can fit the proportions of a rectangular plot very well.

(c)

aquatic plants that need to photosynthesize
and maintain the dissolved oxygen level in
the water. It is true that too much sunlight
encourages algae to increase, giving rise
to problems with 'green water'. This,
however, can be easily resolved by making
sure that the water's surface is well shaded
by the foliage of floating plants and water-
lilies. Some protection from draughts and
prevailing winds is also important to prevent damage to the lush foliage of many
water plants. You should avoid siting a pool
too close to a boundary as this makes
construction and maintenance difficult. If
you are planning to include some kind of
moving water feature, proximity to a source
of power should also be considered.

Ideally, the pool should fit the natural
contours of your garden or patio plan. To
get some idea of the possibilities, it helps to
map out some shapes on the ground using

*Plants in this formal pool have been
limited to only a few species to maintain
its architectural impact. Too many
rampant pool-edge plants would have
ruined the important shape and relevance
of the feature.*

A series of weirs is an attractive way to incorporate moving water into a more formal garden or patio design.

pegs and string or, for informal shapes, a length of hosepipe. This can be viewed from different points around the garden, or from an upstairs window to see if it works.

Size and Style

Lack of space need not limit your water garden ideas; a small pool is just as enjoyable as a large one, it just does not offer the same scope of possibilities for planting and additional features. A traditional pool with a good range of wildlife and plants needs to be at least 180 × 120cm (6 × 4ft) with a minimum depth of 60cm (2ft). If space is really limited, however, you can create a miniature pond in a barrel or urn, complete with fish and miniature plants.

An informal pond should aim to look as natural as possible, so the shape will be naturally contoured with areas for growing a good range of marginal and bog plants ensuring it blends well with its surroundings.

A formal pool edged in stone or brick will be the focal point of a lawn or patio and is usually rectangular, square or circular. Where there is a change of level, this style of pool lends itself to two or even several pools, at different heights, possibly linked by a cascade or spout of water. The raised pool is a useful feature in itself, especially where excavations would be too costly or impractical, and is particularly suited to wheelchair users. Water plants create a rather lush, rampant atmosphere, so their use in the formal water garden is usually limited to a few species or to specimens planted in containers stood near, or on, the pool surround so that they can be controlled more easily.

Ponds and pools are equally adaptable to whatever style of garden you are planning. They are a classic in the traditional garden, maybe incorporating a fountain or statue. The country garden must have its wildlife pond, and the formal ornamental scheme its decorative pool. If you would like to incorporate oriental elements into your garden this is also a theme into which water fits easily. If a large natural pool with a shingle beach and reflected maples is not possible, perhaps you could design a shining stone bowl of water and a trickling water spout in a Japanese style courtyard, which would fit the smallest space and would even suit a balcony or roof garden.

Preparing the Site

Once you have decided on the size and shape of your pond or pool, it should be mapped out accurately using 30cm (12in) pegs and string. Formal shapes will have to be drawn up using a set-square and straight-edge to create an accurate geometric figure. You can make yourself an oversized set-square for accurate right angles by nailing three lengths of wood together to form a triangle in the ratio 3:4:5. Circular or oval shapes are drawn using a centre peg and string: use two fixed stakes and a peg fixed in a loop of string for describing an oval. For irregular, informal ponds a length of hose-pipe or pegs and string should approximate the shape you need. Make sure you do not have any narrow necks or inlets as these

A large informal pond can include a full range of plants from lilies and other aquatics to interesting marginals and moisture-loving species.

do not look right and make construction difficult.

When you are satisfied that the shape is ·right, you can begin to excavate. First any grass must be stripped off in turves which can be used again, either to edge the pond or elsewhere in the garden. This is done by cutting the turves into long strips using a sharp-edged spade and rolling them up, root-side out. Keep them damp until needed. Next remove the topsoil and also store this where it can be re-used around the garden. You can now excavate the subsoil to the required depth: the ideal is between 60–120cm (2–4ft), with the sides angled at about 20 degrees. You should include a shelf for marginal plants about 25cm (10in) below the final level of the water and about 30cm (12in) wide. It is important to ensure that the sides are level. The best way to do this is to drive a 1.2m (4ft) post into the centre and balance a straight-edge between this and one of your perimeter pegs with a spirit-level on top as you go round.

Only the smallest of pools will be practical to dig out by hand. You will probably need a mechanical digger, which can be hired by the day or weekend depending on how big the job is. There are various types of machine, from a dumper-mounted back hoe which will dig to a maximum depth of 1.5m (5ft) and can be operated quite easily, to a JCB which will cope with the largest excavations and requires a trained driver to operate it. You must make sure that you have suitable access for such machines: they may have to be lifted over a fence or wall using a crane which will increase the cost. You should also have some idea before you start of where you are going to put the excavated soil: with an informal pool, a rockery area behind the pool which can be developed into a waterfall will solve this problem. When the pond has been excavated by whatever means and you have checked that it is level, any stones or sharp objects must be removed and all bumps or hollows smoothed out.

Lining a Pond

Concrete

Traditionally ponds were lined with concrete and this is still a strong, watertight option. Concrete has the advantage that it cannot rip or tear and it looks good when building formal features. There is a risk of the concrete cracking in freezing conditions, although chemical additives are available to make this less likely, and you can repair a cracked pool if you drain and empty it. However, it does need some skill to apply concrete if you have not had experience working with it before. Never

Some people don't like the pungent scent, but no-one can resist the wonderful show of shape and colour produced by French marigolds (*Tagetes*) in beds and borders, tubs, pots and all types of container. The bushy plants make a cushion of deep green feathery foliage smothered in little golden 'lion's head' flowers which come in a tremendous variety of different forms. Colours vary from lemon yellow and deep gold through to burgundy red with all manner of interesting combinations and markings. The plants flower freely and can be relied on to make a fine display right through summer and autumn.

tackle concreting if the weather is frosty or too warm and dry.

Cover the excavated area with 19mm (¾in) new (not rusty) chicken-wire, ·tied together with steel ties. A straight-sided pool will need shuttering: this is made from 1–3cm (½–1in) left-over timber and should stand about 10cm (4in) from the sides using 5 × 5cm (2 × 2in) stakes.

To calculate how much concrete you need, add the total surface area of the sides to that of the base and multiply by the thickness, that is 15cm (6in). Make up a mix of one part cement, three parts sand, to six parts aggregate adding any waterproofing and frostproofing chemicals as you mix to a thick consistency with clean water. A concrete mixer will be necessary for all but the smallest pools. Apply the concrete to the sides and base of the pool using a trowel, mixing it well into the chicken-wire. It is important that the mixture is stiff enough not to slump to the bottom of the pond and that the concrete is at least 10cm (4in) thick on the sides to withstand the force of the water. For a neat finish at the top, the concrete can be recessed into the bank with a 7.5cm (3in) notch.

Remove any levelling pegs before the concrete is fully dry and smooth to a fine finish using a float. The slower the concrete dries, the stronger it will be, so protect it from sun, rain or frost by covering it with a tarpaulin. You can fill the pool with water as soon as the concrete is hard to the touch, but you cannot stock it with plants or fish for three months until the poisonous lime in the cement is no longer a risk. You can speed up this process by emptying and refilling the pool three or four times over a period of several weeks, or by completely painting the concrete with a special sealant.

Other Lining Materials

A more popular lining for pools is either a pre-cast shape or a flexible liner, both of

Impatiens (Busy Lizzie) is one of the most popular summer bedding plants for softening the edge of pots, tubs and baskets. It makes a small, compact, bushy plant that produces such a mass of flowers the foliage is almost completely hidden. *Impatiens* will thrive in sun or semi-shade to produce a blaze of colour all summer, making it a patio favourite. There is such a wide range of colours to choose from, too, making this an easy plant to co-ordinate with other bedding material: you should easily be able to find every shade of white, purple, red, orange, pink and mauve to suit your scheme.

which are available in a choice of grades that affect their longevity: basically the more you pay, the longer it will last.

Pre-cast fibreglass moulds are available in a wide range of sizes and shapes and, if you do not mind being restricted to what you can find, these can be a good choice for a quick and easy installation. The hole is excavated to the shape of the mould, allowing 5cm (2in) extra depth and 10cm (4in) extra width and length. A 5cm (2in) blinding layer of damp sand is added all round, after checking for sharp stones, and the pool carefully lowered in, checking that the top is absolutely level using a spirit-level. Any gaps are packed with damp sand.

Flexible liners are made from PVC (polyvinyl chloride) or, tougher and longer lasting, rubber butyl material and are ideal for all types of pool. To calculate how much liner you need, add the length and width of the pool to twice the maximum depth; there is no need to allow for the marginal shelf as the liner will stretch to fit. When the excavations are completed, you must line the pool with special pond insulation or old newspapers to protect the liner. The liner is then laid over the pool and anchored to the sides using large boulders or similar smooth stones. Begin to fill the pool slowly through a hosepipe and the weight of the water will gradually pull the liner into place. As this happens, you should help by folding and tucking any surplus material. When the pool is full, you can cut away any excess leaving about 30cm (12in) on the banks to be concealed beneath your chosen edging material.

Raised Pools

Raised pools are often circular or oval in shape to withstand the pressure of water, although rectangular and square figures are also frequently seen. You need something strong to stand up to that pressure, so concrete is the preferred material for raised pools, although pre-formed fibreglass can be used provided it can be given a stable support. The finished pool is usually faced in stone or brick to match surrounding features.

Sink and Tub Pools

Any container is suitable for creating a miniature pool, provided it can be waterproofed. It should be at least 23cm (9in) deep, and even then you will have to overwinter fish and plants indoors as the water will freeze.

Some containers, like old sinks (with the plug blocked), are naturally waterproof, others can be easily lined with butyl material as described above.

A waterproofed barrel makes an excellent miniature raised pool for the patio.

Bog Gardens

Where a pool is not practical — standing water is not safe for children under five years old, for example — but you would still like to grow a range of interesting marginal or moisture-loving plants, a bog garden is the answer. A bog or marsh area can also be used as a complementary feature adjoining or close to a pond or pool, provided it is no bigger than 10 to 15 per cent of the total surface area of the pool.

A natural depression in the garden is ideal, or you could even create a bog garden in a tub or barrel and sink it up to its rim in the ground. Otherwise, excavate the area to a depth of about 35cm (14in) and line it with butyl, punctured with small drainage holes to maintain the effect of waterlogged soil. A length of pipe punctured with holes and inserted in the bottom of the bog with the other end concealed in nearby foliage is a good way to keep the compost moist in dry weather.

Pond Edgings

Once installed, your pond will need some kind of edging material for a neat finish and to hide any evidence of the liner. The choice is wide according to what kind of effect and atmosphere you are hoping to achieve. Informal pools can use a mixture of grass, random stone or pebbles running gently down a sloping beach into the water. For more formal effects, the pool can be surrounded by brick, paving or timber-decking (*see* Chapter 2) to blend with other features in the garden.

Moving Water Features

The addition of an electric pump means that you can extend your water feature ideas to include moving water, either as an attractive focal point within a pool or as a small feature in its own right. The sparkle and splash of a fountain, cascade or waterfall certainly has a magical quality, and if you do not have room for a pool in the garden a small fountain feature on the patio is a good substitute.

There are two types of pump: surface pumps which operate from outside the water but need dry housing such as a nearby waterproof box or container, and underwater or submersible pumps which are positioned on a permanent level surface in the pool or water reservoir. Submersibles are easier to maintain and more economical to run, but the surface pumps tend to be more powerful. Check with your stockist that your pump is suitable to run the feature you have in mind, especially if you are planning to run a fountain and a waterfall off the same pump using a T-piece connection to the outlet pipe. Generally, the larger submersible types can produce an output of up to 4,500 litres (1,000 gallons) per hour with a head of water (that is, the height of the cascade above the water level) of about 1m (3ft).

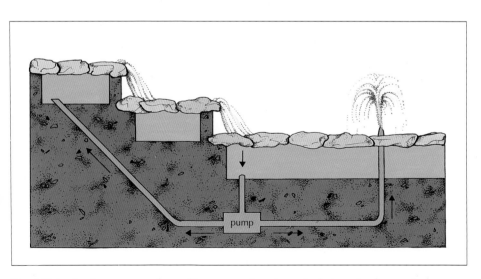

The right sized surface pump can be used to run several moving water features simultaneously. Here a fountain and watercourse are powered by a single pump.

Fountains

From an abstract water sculpture to a pool spray or patio water spout, fountains have the ability to delight and relax the observer. They are easily erected simply by connecting a pump to the relevant fountain nozzle or jet via a length of plastic tubing using jubilee clips. Importantly, the pool or water reservoir should not be less than twice the height of the proposed fountain jet. Nor

An ornate free-standing fountain makes an eye-catching feature for a lawn or patio.

Pretty Primula denticulata *are set against the dramatic backdrop of a large vertical cascade.*

must the water be allowed to splash over the sides of the pool, as this will damage your pool surround and quickly deplete the water.

Particularly attractive for smaller areas is a bubble fountain which operates via a concealed reservoir underground, sending a constant bubble of water over an old millstone, a marble or iron ball, or an arrangement of large pebbles.

Waterfalls and Cascades

A waterfall or cascade makes an interesting change of level in the garden with the added pleasure of the sight and sound of running water. A natural rocky waterfall can take some time to construct: the stones or boulders must be rearranged until they look as realistic as possible. Large rocks usually look better than smaller ones and they should be laid with consideration of their natural strata if they are to look right. Tilt the stones slightly backwards when they are bedded in. Butyl liner behind the rocks will prevent loss of water down the back. Because the water does tend to flow down

A change of level within a patio pool design enables you to link the pools via a small cascade.

the back of the stones, you will need to add a perspex or stone 'lip' at the head of the falls if you want more of a curtain effect. The same principles can be adapted to more formal cascades and weirs on the patio or in the formal garden. A wall, steps or link between two raised pools can be designed to match the materials of surrounding features and be an integral part of the design.

Streams and Watercourses

A winding stream or formal watercourse can make an interesting architectural feature, used either to create a boundary between different parts of the garden or to link certain features. It need not be wide or deep: a depth of 4cm (1½in) can be enough to provide the pleasant sight of water bubbling along over a bed of pebbles.

You construct a stream or watercourse in the same way as a pool, with the banks kept strictly level. A pump is used to recirculate the water and must be powerful enough to pump the water up to the top of the stream before it empties. Informal streams can include exciting marginal plants along the banks or perhaps a simple rustic bridge such as a log or stone slab; a formal watercourse might be edged with brick or stone and incorporate small weirs for interest.

8 • SEATING AND EATING

The patio is truly an outdoor living area and should be furnished accordingly. Your life-style will dictate the kind and style of furniture features you should be considering: comfortable furniture for relaxing, a practical table and seating for dining alfresco, perhaps a barbecue for delicious charcoal-grilled lunches and supper parties. All these features can be purchased in a wide range of styles and price brackets. However, seating and barbecues can also be built in to become an integral part of your patio plan. This not only looks very stylish, but because such features are weatherproof or sheltered, building-in resolves the problem of where to store them during the winter.

Furniture

For relaxing in the sun, the traditional deck-chair is cheap and cheerful with the added advantage that it folds away for easy storage. At the other end of the scale, you may prefer to treat yourself to a fully upholstered

Topiary-trained shrubs in ornamental urns have transformed this simple seating area into a mini feature in its own right.

Stone garden furniture has the advantage that it can be left out all year round with very little maintenance.

lounger, complete with matching foot-stool and drinks trolly. Large, expensive items like this will need dry storage in a shed, garage or summer-house when not in use, so do make sure they fold away or you have the room before indulging yourself.

Garden dining furniture is available in an equally wide choice of styles. Victorian style wrought-metal tables and chairs are attractive and can be left out in all weathers. They are particularly suited to small patios where a circular table and a few chairs seem to take up hardly any room. The only maintenance they need is a rub-down and re-paint when the paint begins to peel.

Stone furniture is another all-weather option and while the seats are not very comfortable for long leisurely meals, they can be quite ornate with moulded decoration. Add brightly coloured cushions for a softer sit.

Some patio furniture is almost smart enough to grace the dining room indoors: hardwood chairs and tables are available in a wide range of styles and, again, are tough enough to be left out so you can use them on fine winter days too. You can also buy hardwood bench seats which are perfect for positioning near a pool, in an arbour or at the end of a path. Some of the more decorative types make a fine focal point against a trellis or backdrop of greenery. To keep them looking in top condition, teak and iroko only need to be cleaned with white spirit and scrubbed with soap and water once a year, then treated with teak oil. Beech and elm furniture should be rubbed down with fine sandpaper and given a generous application of linseed oil.

If you have storage space to put the furniture into at the end of the season there are many types of sturdy plastic patio furniture at both ends of the price scale. Chairs are reasonably comfortable, especially when lavishly upholstered, and you can often buy matching parasols and other accessories. It is a good idea to check that

A traditional bench seat in a sunny position not only affords pleasant views of the garden, but makes a fine focal point itself.

A patio complex may need several different seating areas with furniture for dining or lounging.

the chairs are stackable for space-saving storage.

An excellent piece of furniture for family meals in the garden is the wooden picnic seat with integral table and bench seating. This can be placed on the lawn or patio and is relatively inexpensive to buy, or quite easy to make yourself. You simply have to rub-down and re-varnish or re-oil once a year depending on the type of wood used.

If you are interested in constructing your own garden furniture, built-in bench seating makes an excellent integrated patio feature. It could be incorporated into a corner or used to partition off part of a large patio, maybe back-to-back with a raised pool or planting bed. All kinds of combinations are possible: the concept of integrating planting beds and seating is a lovely one, especially if you plant up the beds with scented species like herbs.

Construct the base of the seating units in concrete in the same way as any other raised patio feature, using them to create a rectangular, circular or even a hexagonal enclosed area around a table. These units can be topped with wooden slatted seats. If you make these hinged or removable, the bases can be used for the storage of cushions, garden games, barbecue utensils, and so on. Alternatively, leave parts of the unit uncovered to be filled with soil to make planting areas. You can make table tops from any waterproof material: an old marble slab, painted concrete, brick or ceramic tiles. Look out for old trestle sewing machines: the wrought-iron base makes a wonderful stand for an outdoor table.

Barbecues

Food always seems to taste better outdoors and a barbecue area is ideal for enjoying the unique flavour of charcoal grilling. It makes sense to position it on a patio or paved area close to your outdoor eating area. If this cannot be near to the house for the convenience of bringing food and drink in and out of the kitchen, make sure that there is safe, dry access via a path or stepping-stones.

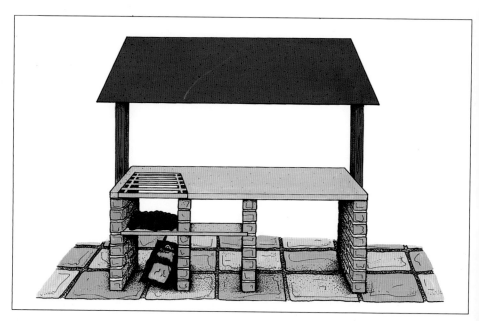

If you eat outdoors regularly you might like to build yourself a barbecue complex complete with shelter, shelves and food preparation area.

If you plan to have frequent barbecues it is worth designing a proper area for it. This should be out of any draughts and not too close to overhead branches that will shed leaves and twigs over your barbecue. You might like to include a counter area for preparing food or even a chimney over a permanent cooking area to reduce the amount of smoke. A novel idea is to build a sunken barbecue area: a paved circle can incorporate built-in seating around the perimeter with a barbecue in the centre.

Types of Barbecue

There are many types of free-standing barbecue suited to different needs and skills. Some must be stored when not in use, but you could always create a special area for the equipment: a level, hard surface with a wooden palisade or screen to protect it from draughts.

The simplest type of barbecue is a grill with a small round or square bowl, which is either floor-standing or fitted with long legs. To save squatting at the floor-standing models, you could custom-build a counter or platform, perhaps with dry storage below to take the barbecue. This type of barbecue is easy to use and ideal for cooking for two or three, but for more sophisticated meals and larger numbers you need something like a kettle barbecue which looks like a giant hamburger bun on legs. This can cope with cooking large amounts of food, even a whole turkey.

If you like the idea of a barbecue but are reluctant to tackle the mess and bother of buying and cooking on charcoal, you can always treat yourself to a gas-powered barbecue. This is fuelled by bottled propane gas but can still offer that smoky charcoal flavour by means of special rocks over which the food is cooked. Gas-powered barbecues can be fairly sophisticated and some offer better facilities than the average kitchen: spit, rotisseries, corn roaster,

A permanent brick or stone barbecue is easily built-in using a standard kit which supplies all the necessary grids and utensils.

kebab attachment, even a preparation surface, bottle rack, a roof overhead and storage shelves.

All these facilities might be incorporated into your own built-in barbecue complex with the barbecue itself gas or charcoal powered. You can buy do-it-yourself kits for charcoal models that include all the necessary racks, charcoal grids and baseplate for collecting the ash. They usually fit into a three-sided brick structure which you build yourself, about 1.2m (4ft) long and at a convenient height for cooking. You should choose solid concrete blocks for the basic construction, not the lightweight type as they are not sufficiently heatproof, and ideally the 23 × 23 × 31cm (9 × 9 × 12in) size. You will only need about eight blocks for a simple barbecue, plus a 5cm (2in) thick 60 × 100cm (2 × 3ft) paving slab to act as the hearth. This basic design can be expanded and embellished into a larger complex if you like, complete with permanent chimney, bench seating and counter preparation areas. An overhead shelter is useful to shade the barbecue cook from sunshine or rain.

GLOSSARY

Aggregate Stony parts mixed with cement, sand and water to make concrete.
Algae Simple organisms which thrive in light, warm conditions and cause pond water to look bright green where its natural ecological balance may have broken down.
Aquatic Plant capable of living with its roots, stems and sometimes leaves submerged in water.

Backfilling Adding soil, hardcore or sand to bring an area up to the desired level.
Basket weave Arrangement of bricks, timber, threads and so on to resemble the woven pattern of a basket.
Bearers Load-bearing timbers used in the construction of timber-decking, pergolas and so on.
Bevelled A sloped edge, on timber, for example, to give a neat finish.
Bog Area of permanently damp soil.
Bobcat Small earth-moving machine useful for pond building.
Bubble fountain Low bubbling fountain effect created using a pump concealed in an underground reservoir of water.
Butyl Type of rubber often used as a pool lining material.

Chlorine Chemical used to sterilize water.
Coach bolts Heavy-duty bolts used for timber.
Compost Potting mixture made either from peat or coconut fibre known as soil-less compost; or from sterilized soil, known as loam compost.
Countersink Sinking the head of a bolt or screw below the surface of the timber.
Course Continuous, usually horizontal layer of building material such as bricks.
Crazy paving Random arrangement of broken paving materials.

Datum peg Measuring peg to which all other pegs refer.
Deciduous Plants which lose their foliage annually.

Decking Continuous timber surface raised off the ground.
Dowel Plug or peg used to join two pieces of timber.
Drystone wall A wall constructed from stone without mortar between the stones.
Dumper mounted back hoe Small earth-moving machine useful for excavating features such as a pool.

Evergreen Plants which retain their foliage throughout the year.

Fertilizer Chemical that provides plant food.
Focal point Centre of attention or the feature which commands the most attention.
Fungicide Chemical used to control fungal diseases.

Gazebo Type of open summer-house or pavilion.
Geometric Composed of simple forms such as circles, rectangles, triangles, and so on.
Gravel Mixture of rock fragments and small pebbles.

Half-hardy Plant usually killed by frost.
Hardcore Broken brick, stones and other rubble used as the footings before laying concrete, and so on.
Hardy Plant tolerant of low temperatures.
Herring-bone Pattern used in brickwork and textiles where two or more rows of short parallel strokes slant in alternate directions to create a series of parallel zigzags.
Hot tub Large wooden barrel fitted with seats and connected to a pump, filter, heater and bubble equipment.

Joists Parallel timbers used to support boards such as timber-decking.

Landscaping Laying out a garden, usually in imitation of natural features; or integrating a new feature into an existing design.

Marginal Plant which grows in the shallows of a pool or stream, or in waterlogged soil.

Marginal shelf Shallow shelf built into the side of a pool where marginal plants can be planted or stood in special baskets.

Masonry bolt Expanding rawlbolt for extremely strong fixing of timber, usually' into stone or brickwork.

Mortar Mixture of cement or lime, or both, with sand to create a bond between bricks or stones.

Mulch Material such as stones, plastic or bark spread on the surface of the soil around a plant to conserve moisture and suppress weeds.

Orientation Position in relation to the points of the compass, that is, north, south, east, west.

Pergola Horizontal trellis or framework sometimes creating a walkway and designed as a support for climbing plants.

Photosynthesis Process used by plants where energy is absorbed by chlorophyll from sunlight.

Pier Column support for a bridge, arch or pergola.

Pointing The cement between bricks or slabs.

Porous Able to absorb water.

Prostrate Creeping along the ground.

Pump Device for raising or moving water.

Rustic Simple, country style.

Screed board A tool used for levelling mortar.

Shingle Small round pebbles sometimes used as a surface material.

Shuttering Timber used to construct a temporary support for wet concrete.

Species Subdivisions of a plant genus.

Spirit-level Tool for checking that a vertical or horizontal surface is completely level.

Straight-edge Piece of straight, unwarped timber used to maintain a straight line.

Submersible Underwater.

Subsoil Layer of soil beneath the surface soil and above the bedrock.

Symmetrical Having two sides perfectly balanced.

Tender Plant which requires protection from low temperatures.

Terracotta Hard, unglazed earthenware.

Topiary Trimming, or training trees and shrubs into ornamental shapes.

Topsoil Fertile soil on top of the ground.

T-piece T-shaped connection used to join three different pieces.

Trellis Structure of latticework useful for supporting plants.

Weir Dam built across a stream or river and designed to raise the water level upstream.

Width gauge Piece of timber used to space slabs or bricks evenly.

INDEX